Th

How the elites divide and control us, and how we could turn the tables on them

Elliot "Alu" Axelman

Alu Axelman

Also by Alu Axelman

The Blueprint For Liberty
Articles of Secession
The Plague That Must Not Be Questioned
The Progressive Solution
Presumed Guilty
Taxation Is Theft

© 2023
All rights reserved

They Fear Unity

Chapter 1: Introduction..7
Chapter 2: The Race War..10
Chapter 3: Class Warfare..32
Chapter 4: Heterophobia..41
Chapter 5: Republicans vs. Democrats......................54
Chapter 6: Corona-Fascism...65
Chapter 7: The Ultimate Divider................................84
Chapter 8: Family, Religion, & Gathering.................95
Chapter 9: Generational Hatred 105
Chapter 10: Enviro-Fascism vs. Humanity...............111
Chapter 11: The Exception To The Rule 132
Chapter 12: How United Are We?..............................136
Chapter 13: Unity Through Division........................146

Foreword

We all know the old saying, attributed to Julius Caesar, "Divide and conquer." The opposite is a better idea: "Unite and win." In this book, THEY FEAR UNITY, Axelman lays out what tactics the Control Freaks use to divide us and he provides a roadmap for how we can come together to build a better future.

As a leader in the Free State movement in New Hampshire, I attend a lot of rallies and protests. I like to maximize my time, so years ago, I put some thought into evergreen protest signs to grab-and-go when the opportunity arises. One of them was: THEY FEAR UNITY.

Why? Because it is true, easy to understand, and gives us an immediate, implementable solution: UNITY. We've all heard the saying, the enemy of my enemy is my friend. If we can set aside our differences enough to shun the Control Freaks and focus on what unites us—our common humanity, our values of live and let live—we will win.

"Human rights" is a concept that needs to make a comeback. Human rights. Not gay rights, not women's rights, not men's rights, not anything other than basic universal HUMAN RIGHTS. The ones we all share, the ones that unite us all.

Freedom of the individual gives freedom to the group. If the smallest minority, the individual, isn't free, humanity cannot be.

Our daily lives are now designed to sow outrage, fear, and envy. Social media keeps us in a heightened, permanent state of alarm. We are divided based on race, class, sexual preference, political parties, our medical choices, even our very genders are now weaponized.

In each chapter of this book, Axelman lays out a subject area where the Control Freaks are trying to divide us, and offers hope for why they will fail.

But in the end, it is up to us.

Have you seen the cartoon of a single politician standing at the end of a plank hanging over a chasm with a crowd standing on the other end? The only thing keeping that suit-and-tie from falling to his death is the people weighing down the opposite end. The time has come for us to walk away. The time has come to plunge the Control Freaks into the abyss of irrelevance.

In order to heal the world, we must walk away from adding to the division, the outrage, the noise. You must reclaim your attention and decide whether you are contributing to unity or division. You need to analyze where you are expending time and energy, because that is your reality, that is the world you are building. Instead of continuing to play the dividers' games, play ours, and win.

Remember, the power of the people is stronger than the people in power. It is up to each one of us to help our common humanity flourish by spreading love not hate, unity not division. In these pages, you will find suggestions for how, together, we can and will win.

Find your tribe and find peace. I have, and I hope you will join me in choosing the side of love.

Carla Gericke, Esq.
President Emeritus, Free State Project
Author of The Ecstatic Pessimist
CarlaGericke.com

Chapter 1: Introduction

It does not take an especially high level of intellect or expertise in political science to understand the strategy of 'divide and conquer'. It is common knowledge that dividing an enemy makes them much easier to defeat. If a potential opposition force is busy fighting itself, you are unlikely to be as vulnerable as you'd be against a united and focused opponent. What's not so well known is that the primary desire of politicians is to control and abuse us; the only use they have for people like you and me is to serve their desires. We produce value with our labor, and they take at least half of our earnings, using the money to enrich themselves and their cronies and to keep us under ever-stricter control.

The more politically astute individuals understand that we are not represented[1] at all by the politicians in Washington D.C. Politicians bribe us for our votes with our own tax dollars, abuse us for two years, and then return to town begging for our vote again come election time. And the cycle repeats, ad infinitum. Even at the highest levels of support, only around 25% of eligible voters actually vote for the candidate who is ultimately declared by the government as the 'duly elected' winner and rightful ruler over all of us. This includes the 75% or 99% of people who voted against the politician.

Why haven't the people fought back and thrown off the government if so many know that the government is malevolent, incompetent, illegitimate, and violates our natural rights on a regular basis?

The simple answer is that politicians have consistently deflected our contempt toward them. Instead of being angry with all politicians or with the government in general, nearly every citizen in the united states is now primarily angry at members of the opposition party or other groups that look or behave differently. Instead of hating the concept of government, Republicans hate the Democrats and believe that the world would be perfect if only Republicans (you know, the great champions of liberty like McConnell, Boehner, Christie, and Cornyn) were in charge. Instead of hating the concept of government, Democrats hate the Republicans and believe that the world would be perfect if only Democrats (fine champions of equality like Biden, Clinton, Schumer, Newsom, Cuomo, Deblasio, and Pelosi) were in charge.

Of course, these beliefs are ridiculous, because even their own leaders do not actually support the policies that their supporters desire. Democrat politicians don't care about foreign interventionism, police accountability, or cannabis, and Republican politicians don't care about gun rights, economic freedom, or school choice. They just know how to pretend to support what's popular among their respective political bases.

How exactly have politicians successfully kept us so divided for so long?

What can "We The People" do about the division fueled by evil politicians?

How can we unite, at least for long enough to aim our frustration at the politicians?

Is our precious union unraveling at the seams??

I will seek to answer these questions and many more in the pages ahead.

Chapter 2: The Race War

In addition to being the party of racism since its inception, the Democrat Party has been utilizing a race-focused agenda to divide and conquer the American people for decades. Unbeknownst to many young Americans, the Ku Klux Klan[2] was created as a sort of enforcement arm of the Democrat Party, generally targeting Blacks and Republicans[3] with their attacks. The members of this racist group judged and punished people for immutable characteristics, such as the color of their skin.

Sound familiar?

Increasingly over the past few years, Democrats in positions of power have focused on the color of each person's skin and encouraged their followers to do the same. Today, anyone who makes statements to the effect of *"I look to a day when people will not be judged by the color of their skin, but by the content of their character"*[4] is considered a racist and a bigot, irony be damned. Democrats and their supporters now believe that everyone MUST be judged by the color of their skin and Whites should be judged as inherently evil, simply because their skin has less melanin than their Black counterparts.

In recent years, cities and states ruled by progressives have begun to bring back segregation. This time, it is against White people, and it is receiving little negative attention. King County Library in the State of Washington is segregating White people because they are less desirable than the other races. After being caught red-handed[5] holding segregated training sessions, the government-run institution denied the accusation. The City of Seattle also segregates[6] White employees during training sessions. Columbia University has begun to segregate its graduation ceremonies[7]. White people are considered so despicable that they cannot even participate in the same graduation as Black people. That is the type of division that the radical left has created.

In 1961, Democrat President, John F. Kennedy mandated via executive order[8] that all institutions that contract with the federal government or receive any federal funds (which includes nearly every large company and college) to *"take affirmative action to ensure that applicants are employed, and that employees are treated during employment, without regard to their race, creed, color, or national origin."* This was the beginning of the racist calamity know as 'affirmative action'[9].

In 1964, Congress passed the 'Civil Rights Act'[10], further cementing into law the racist policy requiring colleges and employers to treat Black people better than their White counterparts, which ironically contradicts the 14th amendment's 'equal protection clause'.

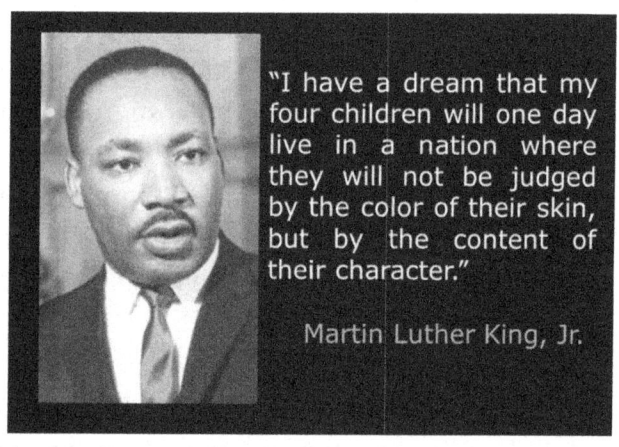

"I have a dream that my four children will one day live in a nation where they will not be judged by the color of their skin, but by the content of their character."

Martin Luther King, Jr.

This quote is considered to be racist in today's world, because it denies that people should be treated based on skin color

Since then, the policy has grown more tyrannical and divisive, and it now harms people of all races. The policy was challenged in court in 1978[11], when a qualified applicant sued UC Davis Medical School[12] for rejecting his application based on his skin color – because he was White. The school admitted that they did not care about how qualified the applicants were – they reserved 16% of their seats for non-Whites. So, even if the 100 most qualified applicants happened to be White, they would choose at least 16 Black candidates over the White ones in order to satisfy the 'racial justice' agenda. Which students actually deserved to be accepted? Who would make the best doctors? Oh, that's not important! All that matters is that White people are punished and Black people are rewarded!

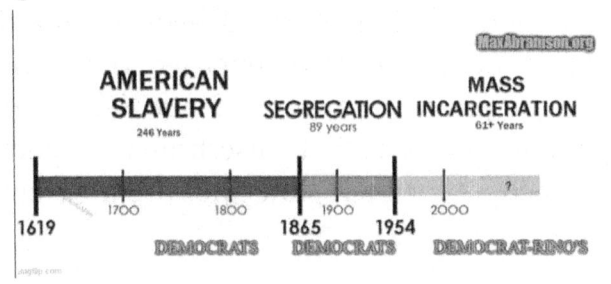

```
                                           MaxAbramson.org
            AMERICAN                    MASS
            SLAVERY   SEGREGATION   INCARCERATION
            246 Years    89 years      61+ Years

      |————————————|———————|———|——————————?
   1619     1700      1800   1865  1954   2000
                          DEMOCRATS  DEMOCRATS  DEMOCRAT-RINO'S
```

In a complicated decision, the Supreme Court ruled 5-4 that colleges accepting federal funds could legally use race as *part* of their admissions process (something that previously was considered 'racism') but that their quota of 16% was too *specific* to be considered non-racist. Therefore, the court determined that the medical school's policy *did* violate Bakke's 14th amendment guarantee of equal treatment.

In 2003, the Supreme Court considered Grutter v. Bollinger[13], another affirmative action case. When a White applicant was rejected by the University of Michigan's law school despite high GPA and LSAT scores because they intentionally reserved seats for Black students, Grutter sued the school for violating his right to equal protection under the law. In another 5-4 decision, the Supreme Court ruled that the school's policy was 'narrowly tailored', and that its anti-White admissions policy was legal and could remain in place. Clarence Thomas, the second Black person to ever sit on the Supreme Court, strongly opposed the court's majority opinion and pointed out the obvious fact that policies that discriminate against White people for their skin color are inherently racist.

Affirmative action hurts White people by keeping them out of colleges and jobs despite their qualifications. But these policies also harm Black people and other minorities by patronizing them. In the 1960s, when Black people were truly gaining their full rights for the first time in their lives, there was a much stronger argument for granting them some advantages. But 60 years later, when their grandchildren have no excuse to be unsuccessful and are generally as fortunate as their White counterparts, affirmative action harms them. The current policy tells normal Black children a discouraging message:

"You are stupid and not capable of success. So, politicians passed laws that will get you into colleges and jobs that you don't really deserve. Remember, you didn't earn it; politicians took these opportunities from White folks and handed them to you. Without the government, you'd have nothing; you couldn't make it on your own!"

I have known many people of all races and from all parts of the world. I've met people who actually moved here from Africa. In high school, nearly all of my friends were Black (in my high school, Whites were the tiny minority). Many of my closest friends today are Hispanic, black, Indian, Irish, and so on. My wife is Asian, and my neighbors, friends, and co-workers are from all over the world. I do not believe that any of these people are less intelligent or capable than I am simply because of the color of their skin. Of course, many of the smartest and most productive people in the world are 'racial minorities'. Interestingly, Whites are statistically a minority of the world's population, if you want to get technical. Sources seem to estimate that there are around 800 million White people[14] in the world, which would represent around 10% of the global population. The White population is also declining rapidly[15], especially relative to other ethnicities.

While I do not believe that Blacks are less capable or less intelligent than Whites, that is precisely what Democrats believe. They often exclaim that Black people are so stupid that they need help getting into college and getting jobs because they can't accomplish those things on their own. The Democrat ideology opposes voter ID laws and openly expresses that Black people are too stupid to obtain a license or other forms of identification. Again, I lived and worked in many Black and Hispanic neighborhoods, and I found that this was not the case. I have hardly met anyone (other than a few homeless people who were mentally ill, on drugs, and mostly White) who did not have an ID card. Here in New Hampshire, a few of my friends have no government-issued ID cards. They are mostly White, and it is an active choice they make as principled anarchists who are determined to interact with the government as little as possible.

Regardless of the facts, radical leftists continue to push the race war. The more they punished White people and the more they patronized Black people, the more the groups would grow to resent each other.

Adding fuel to the race war, leftist colleges began to discriminate against Asians even more than they did against White students! It turns out that Asians are the best students, which caused them to account for a disproportionate number of seats in elite colleges and grad schools. So, colleges had lots of Asians, some Whites, and a few Blacks and Hispanics. This was based on merit, but apparently, merit has no place in the dystopian, leftist, racist society of the united states.

So, colleges began to require Asians to score higher than Whites on their tests in order to be admitted, while Black people were not required to score as high on the admissions tests as their White counterparts. Thus began a race-based, three-tiered system of college admissions in the united states.

In 2014, a group called 'Students for Fair Admissions' sued Harvard University for discriminating against Asians by setting the bar for their admission much higher than applicants of other races. In 2019, a federal judge ruled that Harvard's admissions process was legal. The racist schools may have skirted the law by claiming that their admissions process is 'holistic' and takes into account each applicant's intangible qualities and extracurricular activities and Asians are all boring losers with poor leadership skills, according to the leftist university. Some believe that the case is headed for the Supreme Court within the next few years.

Interestingly, Senate Democrats opposed an amendment[16] that would have prohibited anti-Asian discrimination by colleges receiving federal funds in April of 2021.

In 2023, 17 government-run high schools[17] in Virginia reportedly withheld merit scholarship awards sent from colleges to high school students in order to ensure that no students felt inferior about not earning a college scholarship. Most of the victims were studious Asian-American students, as reported by CNN[18].

Increasingly intense and hateful rhetoric against White people by politicians in recent years has brought about an escalation of anti-White crime. Black people kill White people twice as often[19] as White people kill Black people in the united states. If a White person harms a Black or Hispanic person, it's now front-page news. If a Black person kills a White child, it is largely ignored.

Around 2013, a new fad swept across the nation. It was called the 'knockout game' because teens would punch an unsuspecting stranger as hard as they could when they were not looking, and the goal was to knock them out (or kill them) with a single strike. The perpetrators were nearly all Black, the victims were nearly all white, and many of them were women[20] or elderly. But race didn't matter to the media in these cases, because it didn't align with their agenda. At least four people were murdered by this 'game', and many more were seriously injured. But the anti-white hate was just getting started.

An article published by The Root[21] in 2021 eliminated any pretense regarding the despicable malice that progressives have for White people. Titled 'Whiteness Is a Pandemic', the article attacked White people for their skin color throughout the piece:

"Whiteness is a public health crisis. It shortens life expectancies, it pollutes air, it constricts equilibrium, it devastates forests, it melts ice caps, it sparks (and funds) wars, it flattens dialects, it infests consciousnesses, and it kills people—white people and people who are not white, my mom included. There will be people who die, in 2050, because of white supremacy-induced decisions from 1850."

By 2016, leftist politicians[22] were proudly announcing their plans to redistribute money from White people to their Black neighbors. The concept of 'reparations' continues to grow in popularity among progressives and is likely to evolve into a substantive policy within a few years. According to a 2021 Pew Research poll, 77% of African Americans[23] support reparations while only 18% of Whites support the idea. This means that once reparations become mandatory, White people will grow to resent

Black people so much that tensions could boil over.

In 2019, a federal bill[24] that sought to begin the reparations process had 174 sponsors in the House of Representatives. Joe Biden has indicated his support for reparations[25], despite the fact that no White person alive today has owned slaves, and very few even had distant ancestors involved in slavery 200 years ago. In 2022, a panel established by the San Francisco government officially proposed[26] that the city government give reparations to Black residents in the form of a $5 million payment and the elimination of all their debt[27].

Slavery was never legal in California, unless one considers the harsh prison labor enforced by prominent Democrats like Kamala Harris[28] and Gavin Newsom[29] to be slavery.

During the year 2020, many of the loudest voices on the left insisted that the worst part of the coronavirus pandemic was not that it was killing millions of people or destroying the world economy, but that it was disproportionately affecting minorities[30]. Predictably, these "progressives" used yet another tragedy to push their race-based[31] agenda. Politicians and their cronies in the 'private' medical sector pushed this narrative repeatedly throughout the whole year, finally bringing the idea to a climax: An Antiracist Agenda for Medicine[32]

In early 2021, prestigious hospital systems began to roll out their anti-White policies that would prioritize Black patients and de-prioritize White patients. In other words, the plan is to let White people die[33] in order to accelerate the racial shift throughout the united states (Whites account for a little over 50% of the population, but that number is plummeting). This sentiment was echoed by multiple medical journals and hospitals, including the Lancet[34], the New England Journal of Medicine[35], Massachusetts General Hospital[36], and many others. It's only a matter of time until this cancer spreads to your local hospital. When that happens, make sure to check the 'Black' or 'other' box when they ask you which race you identify with.

Of course, the anti-White racism in medicine[37] should not come as a complete surprise to those who have been paying close attention. When the coronavirus vaccines first became available, each state granted high-priority groups the first opportunity to receive the inoculation. States generally offered the shot to frontline healthcare workers, the elderly, and the sick. Leftist states, however, used the vaccine as yet another opportunity to signal how virtuous and 'anti-racist' they were. So, they offered the shot to Black people[38] and other minorities before offering it to White people. In fact, the CDC said that skin color[39] **should** be taken into account when determining who should get the vaccine first. The report explained that health workers (doctors, nurses, EMTs, etc.) should get the vaccine before the elderly - because health workers are more likely to be Black and Hispanic than the elderly.

"Older populations are whiter, " Harald Schmidt, a professor of ethics and health policy at the University of Pennsylvania, told The New York Times. *"Society is structured in a way that enables them to live longer. Instead of giving additional health benefits to those who already had more of them, we can start to* **level the playing field a bit.***"*

"Level the playing field".

As in, let's kill White people or let them die, because we need to pay them back for their ancestors' racism.

This is what the DC Empire's Centers for Disease Control's advisors think the vaccine administration plan should be based on.

A 2022 report[40] found that 58 of the top 100 medical schools in the union incorporated critical race theory (CRT) into their curriculum. No wonder so many in the health professions are anti-White racists.

Of course, the leftist elites have also made every effort to turn Latin-American immigrants against White people. One example is the pathetic Forbes article[41] decrying evil White Americans for the crime of earning more money than immigrants. The article bashes Wyoming - one of the most White and Republican states - for having the largest wage gap between those born here and those born abroad. The leftist rag failed to mention that immigrants and their children earn as much or more than their American-born counterparts. Even the NY Times[42] acknowledged that the children of immigrants *"were nearly twice as likely to become rich"* as those with parents who were born here. Immigrants are also nearly twice as likely[43]

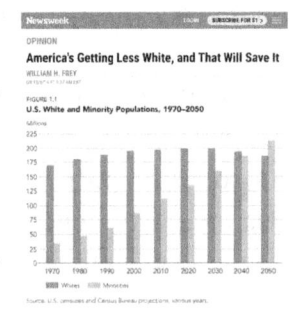

to start their own businesses. Of course, the richest man in the world at the time of this writing is an American who immigrated here from South Africa and started multiple companies.

According to a 2018 study[44] by the National Foundation for American Policy, immigrants founded or co-founded 55% of the billion-dollar companies in the united states.
But those facts are not convenient for the leftists' narrative. So, they neglect to mention them.

All of these policies and propaganda campaigns aim to turn the races against one another. If Blacks, Whites, Hispanics, and Asians are too busy fighting each other, they won't fight the real enemy - politicians. Despite their tremendous efforts and massive amounts of assistance from mainstream media, nearly every school, and just about every other influential institution in the union, the race war has mostly failed.

Throughout the united states, people of all colors increasingly get along with each other and often fall in love with one another. My brothers, my friends, and I have been in relationships with people from nearly every country on Earth, including Pakistan, Afghanistan, the Philippines, Ecuador, Cambodia, Mexico, and many others. We have been with Jews, Christians, Muslims, and atheists. When I was in Ferguson, Missouri at the height of the media-portrayed race war, all I saw was joyful unity between the Black and White residents of the small country town. Despite many leftists believing that Wyoming is racist and White, we found that Jews were welcomed in Cheyenne, and I returned from the bathroom to find my companion flirting with a beautiful Black woman at the bar. I wondered how many young Black women were in Wyoming.

My question was answered during my next visit to Cheyenne when we found ourselves in another bar (it was pretty much a dance club, actually) that primarily played hip-hop and Latin dance music. Nearly everyone in the jam-packed bar was Black or Hispanic, and they were all much better dancers than me. And guess what? Everyone in that bar got along with each other quite well.

The rest of Wyoming is populated by Hispanics, African-Americans, Native Americans, and many others, nearly all of which were color-blind and seemed to have much better things to worry about than racism.

I think I was in North Dakota when we stopped for tacos at a small shop that was run by Mexicans who felt totally at home in their small mountain town, most of which seemed to be White.

My brother and I had similar experiences in every other state we visited. Traveling all over the united states taught me firsthand how colorblind Americans truly are. They certainly are not as racist as CNN had made them out to be! The united states are mostly filled with people who simply do not care to hate others for the color of their skin. Turn off the TV and do some traveling, and you'll see what I mean.

For years, the elites have used police brutality and misconduct to fuel their race war. The typical narrative propagated by progressives in the media has been that *"White cops are hunting down[45] Black people"*. The statistics demonstrate that Black people are not more likely to be killed by White police officers. But these discussions all completely miss the point. Police officers are nothing but violent gangsters who treat people with disrespect and disturbing levels of violence. They do this on a regular basis and with nearly complete impunity. They do this to people of all colors. Personally, I am as white as they come, and cops treat me like filth from the moment they encounter me. I have seen this occur countless times with victims of all ethnicities. That being said, my years of police accountability activism has made me believe that it's possible that many cops treat Black people worse than White people due to prejudice. It should go without saying that acting in a racist and violent manner is despicable. But again, the main issue is that cops treat *people* terribly and are almost never held accountable. Those who focus on how White cops treat Black suspects miss the primary issue. There is a color issue. And it's the armed

≡ The New York Times

OPINION

Jogging Has Always Excluded Black People

Born in lily-white Oregon, it's a sport that's long claimed to be for everyone — even as African-American joggers have been persistently subjected to harassment and worse.

thugs behind the 'thin blue line' against the rest of us non-government employees. All you need to do is listen to any two cops chatting with each other, and you'll quickly realize that they have a strong 'us versus them' mentality. They are important and must never get hurt. Civilians (or 'perps', as cops very often use to refer to innocent individuals they encounter) are a lower class of people and their lives do not matter nearly as much as a cop's life. That is the issue.

In my prior book 'Presumed Guilty', I discuss the primary issues with the American justice system and policing in depth. In the book and in my bookmarks, I have thousands of examples of vicious police brutality caught on video. And we can assume that each of those cases represents a larger number (maybe 50, 100, or 1,000) of cases of police brutality that were not captured by any video. The thugs who call themselves cops seem to murder and rape people on a daily basis. But many people have begun to notice that the media only focuses on the incidents involving white cops and Black victims. Even Kyle Rittenhouse was painted as a horrible white supremacist who ran around killing Blacks. Many Americans did not discover until his trial that the three people he shot in self-defense were all White. The elites' media apparatus used this case and countless others to sow division between the white, conservative, militia types of people and the Black, progressive, and police-accountability

> And then there are masks. The People's C.D.C. strongly supports mask mandates, and they have called on federal, state, and local governments to put them back in place, arguing that "the vaccine-only strategy promoted by the CDC is insufficient." The group has noted that resistance to masks is most common among white people: Lucky Tran, who organizes the coalition's media team, recently tweeted a YouGov survey supporting this, and wrote that "a lot of anti-mask sentiment is deeply embedded in white supremacy."

types of people. As a host on Free Talk Live pointed out on the January 27th, 2023 show, the elites could not allow the BLM and MAGA forces to link arms and direct their fury at the politicians. So, they tactfully divide and control both sides.

Just prior to publishing this book, video footage of an innocent Black man being brutally beaten to death in Memphis surfaced online. Although all five officers involved were Black, the footage was so disturbing and violent that it went viral even without help from the mainstream media. Unable to ignore the evil incident perpetrated by the cop gang, the leftist media[46] simply blamed[47] the murder on white supremacist racism.

They Fear Unity

> **Jeremy Kauffman** ✓
> @jeremykauffman
>
> Google has launched a new campaign called "Buy Black" that encourages people to shop based on the race of the store owner.
>
> Stores in search and map results will be given icons indicating the race of the owner to make this easier.
>
> [video: Buying All Black - Ludacris feat. Flo Milli (A Google #BlackOwnedFriday Anthem)]
>
> 10:39 AM · Dec 15, 2022

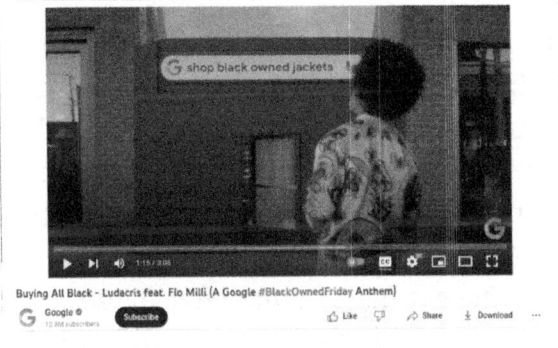

The race war is not going well for the great dividers in Washington DC. People are too social. They are too open-minded. They love making friends, especially with people who look different. No, the race war won't do the trick.

"We need to find a better wedge to drive between the people…"

Chapter 3: Class Warfare

For centuries, authoritarians (which describes about 95% of all elected officials) have been attempting to pit the poor against the rich in an effort to divide and control their constituents.

In the 1930s, President Franklin D. Roosevelt capitalized on the resentment toward hard workers and wealthy Americans. Using the war as an excuse to raise revenue for the government, the socialist Roosevelt told Congress[48] in 1942 that *"no American citizen ought to have a net income, after he has paid his taxes, of more than $25,000 a year."* This leftist hero wanted to raise the rate of the highest income tax bracket to 100%, but he couldn't get Congress to support such a communist policy.

He ultimately issued an *executive order* that limited top corporate salaries to $25,000 after taxes, meaning that if a person earned enough money, their effective federal income tax rate might be 99% of their income! As the war ended, Roosevelt and Congress compromised and lowered the top marginal income tax rate to 94%. This meant that the hardest workers paid an effective federal income tax of 69%. After the other dozens of taxes, these 'evil rich people' may have kept only around 5-10% of their annual earnings.

Since 1945, the top federal income tax rate has decreased to 37%[49], but the dozens of other taxes have quite possibly made up for the decrease. More than perhaps ever before in history, the elites have fomented intense hatred and resentment toward the rich. In 2022, calling someone 'wealthy' is a criticism comparable to calling someone 'evil', 'greedy', or 'corrupt'. Unless, of course, they are socialist or fascist elites like Obama[50], Clinton[51], Gore[52], or a member of BLM (which may stand for 'Burn Loot Murder[53] or Buy Large Mansions[54], depending on whom you ask). Those people can be as rich as they want without being condemned by progressives.

The anti-capitalist and anti-wealth sentiment has grown so toxic that many people are now ashamed of their wealth. Those who wish to be popular or even accepted in polite society often prefer to keep their success hidden, for fear of being ostracized or outed as a 'capitalist pig'. Of course, radical leftists (Marxists) do not understand that without wealthy people, we would have little to no employers, meaning little to no jobs, services, or products.

Politicians and leftists consistently ignore the Laffer curve[55], which illustrates why higher tax rates do not necessarily correlate with higher overall tax revenue for the government. (When you tax people at insanely high rates, they either stop working, avoid taxes, or they move their operations to other countries, totally depriving the government of the tax revenue they would have paid.)

The socialists persisted and continued to employ the class warfare that Karl Marx called for in 1848. The founder of Marxism believed that capitalists were evil and that poor people must fight against the upper class and seize control of the means of production (the economy). Communists believe that the 'collective', meaning the government, should control all resources, property, and businesses and that it should distribute to each person just enough resources to survive (bread lines, housing, free healthcare, etc.) according to their needs. The Communist theory does not allow for the private ownership of any property, including money, weapons, homes, or anything else.

Since politicians (most of whom are Marxists, to varying degrees) began to control nearly all schools in the united states, they have been indoctrinating every student to resent rich people and blame them for all their problems.

Thanks to decades of indoctrination via the government-run education system (which educates 90% of students throughout the union) and leftist allies in the media, churches, Hollywood, and elsewhere, Americans now believe that rich people are evil, greedy, and pay little to no taxes. In surveys, people confidently tell researchers that the rich only pay a tiny fraction[56] of the federal taxes. In reality, the top 1% of earners currently pay 40% of the taxes[57]. The other 99% combined only account for 60% of the federal tax revenue. Still, 64% of respondents[58] told Reuters that the wealthiest people deserve to have some of their money - not annual income - but their actual savings, confiscated by politicians each year.

Democrats like Senator Elizabeth Warren have been increasingly pushing for a wealth tax[59]. In typical communist fashion, these politicians believe that if a person has a large net worth, the government should confiscate a portion of it each year. Never mind that their money is not being stored under their mattress; it's tied up in their businesses that provide jobs for Americans and in banks that loan money to Americans. Socialists like Warren either don't know or don't care how the economy actually works[60].

Over the past few years, progressives have been crusading against 'wealth inequality'. This is simply a rebranded way of convincing naive millennials that rich people are getting richer by abusing the poor, who are growing poorer. Remember: rich people are the cause of all of society's problems!

Is it true that the rich are getting richer and the poor are getting poorer? Not really, but it is true that the most Democratic states do have the worst wealth inequality[61].

According to a study by The Economist[62], the bottom 10% in the united states live better[63] than the top 10% in Mexico, Turkey, Brazil, Portugal, Russia, Israel, and likely, many other countries. Of course, the quality of life for the bottom 10% of Americans is improving each year, as are their opportunities to move into the middle or upper class. Keep in mind that the poorest people in the union now enjoy expensive smartphones, new cars, and so much food[64] that they literally become obese.

Better-life index*
Selected countries, 2013, 1=best

Socioeconomic status of population†:
○ bottom 10%   ○ top 10%

United States	
Canada	
Sweden	
Australia	
Switzerland	
Britain	
Germany	
OECD average	
Poland	
Japan	
France	
Italy	
Israel	
Russia	
Portugal	
Brazil	
Turkey	
Mexico	

Sources: OECD; *The Economist*   *Based on 10 normalised indicators   †Based on income or education

economist.com/graphicdetail

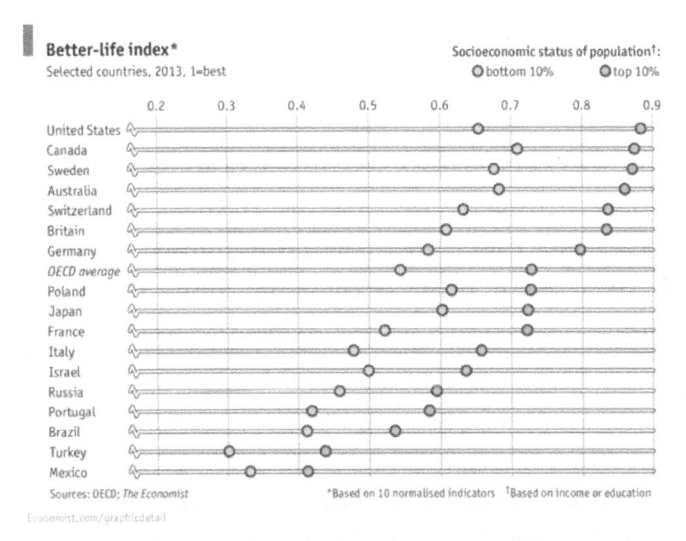

This chart clearly shows that the poorest 10% of Americans have a better quality of life than the average person in other countries.

One of the most important factors at play here is income mobility; how easily people can improve their financial situation and move up to the next quintile. Despite leftist claims[65] that it's impossible for poor people to move up to the working, middle, or upper classes in our horrible, capitalist, racist society, the data shows that it's quite common for poor people to improve their station in the land of 'diminishing opportunity'. Between 1967 and 2009, the real mean household income of the lowest quintile (bottom fifth) increased by 25%[66].

How easy is it for poor people to move into higher quintiles?

From 1987 to 1996, 45% of those in the bottom quintile moved up to a higher quintile. Conversely, 42% of those in the highest quintile fell to a lower bracket over the same ten-year period.

Do children of poor people remain poor forever?

The data from the US Census, the treasury, and the Brookings Institute show that children born to parents in the bottom quintile earn double what their parents earned. Additionally, children in the bottom quintile quadruple[67] their chances of making it to the top quintile if they are born to married parents.

These facts are not exactly top secret. It's common knowledge that kids do better when they have two parents who are married, when they have a house, and when their parents have jobs. Which leads to some compelling questions:

Why do progressives place so much emphasis on destroying the nuclear family? Why encourage single parenthood and discourage marriage if it causes such direct harm to children?

Are you starting to see why the radical left's attempt to create a class war has largely failed?

Americans are not necessarily as stupid as politicians assumed they were (at least not in this instance). They understand very well that they should not support massive taxes on the income or the net worth of the rich for three primary reasons:

1) The rich people are the ones who employ the average and poor people. Without rich businessmen or the potential to become rich, companies would not be able to employ as many people, and would not have the incentive to produce goods or provide services, let alone the incentive to take risks or innovate. If all wealth beyond a certain amount were confiscated by politicians, people would lose motivation to work if it meant that they could not keep what they rightfully earned.

2) Without rich people storing money in banks, the banks would not have much money. Without money, banks can't really loan money to Joe Average and Sally Normal. If Joe can't get

a loan to buy a house (mortgage) and if Sally can't get a loan for her car (financing), they will be negatively impacted by the war against the rich. The banks could create new money as they provide those 'loans', but that would be the definition of inflation of the money supply, which would rob everyone who holds dollars by causing them to lose a large amount of their value.

3) As you now know about economic mobility, Joe and Sally understand that if they support high taxes on the rich, it could hurt them - because they might soon be considered rich! Many people have gone from being poor or average to wealthy. Once you earn more than around $150,000 a year as a household (which is hardly 'rich' if you have a house and children) you are considered to be rich, and you can expect to be taxed at an effective rate of around 50% under current tax laws.

"No...class warfare showed some promise, but we have not convinced all poor people to hate all rich people.....they just want to become rich themselves! Those greedy pigs! We need to find another way to divide them!"

Chapter 4: Heterophobia

One of the more recent tactics that politicians and their cronies have employed in their efforts to divide people involves the LGBT movement. Of course, the "average" gay person themselves is generally not to blame. However, the evil elites have largely co-opted the movement and they now use many in this group as soldiers in their Marxist battles as they wage war against personal liberty.

Over the past few years, the elites have successfully rebranded the movement as 'LGBTQIA+'. By appearing to be as 'inclusive' as possible due to including all non-traditional sexual preferences[68], the elites hope to bring a large percentage of individuals into the fold. This large group could then be deployed as their army to fight against the other side - those damn heterosexual people who are not transgender. The most hateful in this movement have coined slurs for straight people and non-trans people. They condemn straight people as 'hetero' or 'breeder', and they refer to non-trans people as 'cisgender'.

Whenever their opponents (pro-freedom individuals) attempt to make progress, leftist elites dispatch their LGBT activists to defeat the conservatives and libertarians. They accomplish this by simply accusing anyone who does not totally support Marxism of being an anti-LGBT 'bigot'. While a few conservatives surely do not support gay marriage and may in fact be bigoted, the overwhelming majority of pro-freedom individuals have no issues whatsoever with gay people or the LGBT movement at large. Still, the radical left has successfully crafted the narrative as *"anyone who supports gun rights or education rights or lower taxes or anything that is not pure communism clearly hates gay people!"*

Naturally, this causes progressives to hate straight people, which causes straight people to resent LGBT activists, and possibly all gay people. And thus, the war over sexual identity was manufactured.

Over the past few years, leftist elites have brainwashed many of their activists into believing that anyone who believes that straight people are not evil must clearly hate LGBT people and want them to die. Because the owner of the Chick-Fil-A fast food restaurant chain donated to some conservative organizations in the past, leftist activists spent years waging war against his restaurants. When the (previously) conservative Christian restaurant opened a location in Toronto, sociopathic activists conducted a 'die-in' protest[69] in front of the store and made it difficult for customers to enter and exit the establishment. Eventually, the traditionally conservative, pro-life business caved to the leftist mob. Dan Cathy, the CEO of Chick-Fil-A soon began to bow down to the radical left on TV, even going so far as to shine the shoes[70] of Black supremacist activist and rapper, 'Lecrae', who ironically claims to be a devout Christian himself. The rich, old, White, leftist man called on all White people to repent for their inherent racism by shining the shoes of Black men. Dan Cathy also stopped donating[71] to Christian charities that support traditional marriage due to the immense leftist pressure. The radical left won that battle decisively.

Now that the elites have successfully painted straight and 'cis' people as evil, bigoted, second-class citizens to the American public, mainstream websites like Buzzfeed can get away with publishing articles that do nothing but bash straight people[72].

For at least the past decade, many institutions in the united states and around the world have celebrated and commended people for being gay and treated them as superior to their straight counterparts. In 2015, New York City made it a crime to refer to someone with the 'wrong' gender pronouns. Referring to a transgender person by the pronoun that aligns with their biological gender can result in a $250,000 fine[73] in the progressive paradise of NYC. This policy punishes non-trans people for insulting transgender people, while those in the LGBT community are encouraged to condemn and punish straight people. This stokes more resentment between the two groups.

Making it clear that they are the real anti-women movement, progressives have supplanted women and girls in their own sports leagues. Anyone who knows basic biology (so, everyone besides the most radical psychotic leftists) understands that males are generally larger, stronger, and more athletic than females. Men literally have stronger muscles and bones than women. These are facts. It's the reason that sports are divided between the two genders. Women could not compete with men in basketball, football, or fighting sports. I say this as someone who has a fair amount of experience in basketball, football, and martial arts, with both men and women. So, when male teens claim to identify as female and smoke the real girls in the 55-meter dash[74], one could understand why the girls feel crushed. Many girls and women work their asses off training nonstop in order to win races and earn college scholarships for track. And then a boy comes in and wins first place, killing their dreams, due to an unfair biological advantage. Keep in mind that males have eight times more testosterone than females. This naturally occurring hormone is literally a steroid[75] and is considered a performance-enhancing substance.

As one woman explained in a 2020 Newsweek[76] article: *"Consider Felix, a contender for the title of fastest female sprinter in the world, who holds more Olympic medals than even Usain Bolt. Her lifetime best for the 400-meter is 49.26 seconds. Based on 2018 data, nearly 300 high school boys in the U.S. alone could beat it."*

High school boys actually beat the best women in the Olympics in nearly every track & field event, as demonstrated by BoysVsWomen.com[77]. A boys under-15 team actually beat the USA Women's soccer team[78] in a sport that is hardly based on physical strength.

In 2019, a man smashed four female powerlifting records[79].

In 2022, a man won the NCAA women's swimming title[80].

A college basketball star who was too short to make the NBA changed their gender[81] and became a star in the WNBA.

But these examples all pale in comparison to what's occurred in combat sports. In 2014, a man who identified as a woman competed in a mixed martial arts bout with a real woman. The man easily overpowered her and beat the hell out of her, causing the referee to stop the fight after just 39 seconds[82]. The woman suffered a broken skull[83]. Since then, other men[84] have competed in MMA and beaten real women using their natural advantage. Some might speculate about the future of combat sports in a world where people can choose to identify as whatever gender, age, or weight they desire.

The left's sexual revolution has caused intense pushback. In 2019, a female powerlifter named Beth Stelzer created Save Women's Sports[85], *"an organization dedicated to protecting the right of every woman and girl to compete on a level playing field."* Augmented by organizations such as 'Alliance Defending Freedom'[86], 'Independent Women's Voice'[87], 'Concerned Women for America'[88], and many others, the movement to push back against the destruction of female sports by biological males is achieving some success. Over the past two years, the movement helped pass new laws protecting girls from being beaten by male athletes in Texas[89], Florida[90], Idaho[91], Mississippi[92], Arkansas[93], Montana[94], Arizona[95], Iowa[96], Kentucky[97], Tennessee[98], South Carolina[99], Oklahoma[100], Utah[101], Alabama[102], West Virginia[103] and South Dakota[104]. In 2022, the Indiana[105] legislature overrode Governor Holcomb's veto of HB 1041[106], becoming the 17th state in the union to pass a law protecting girl's sports. This success is going to cause even stronger assaults on normalcy by the progressives, further deepening the divide.

Over the past few years, the radical progressives have begun to seriously claim that men can have periods and give birth, too. They believe that normal women who 'identify' as men, even while giving birth to babies, are a clear example of this fact. Because men can also have babies[107], the radical leftists began to redefine[108] those persons as 'birthing people'. Ironically, this new demonym insults real women by distilling them down to their most primitive biological function. Remember when progressives complained about women being treated as nothing more than 'baby factories'? And now, we have come full circle to referring to them as just 'birthing people'. This also insults women by insinuating that men can also give birth, erasing what many women consider to be a special privilege that God granted only to women. The radical leftists have also begun to use the term 'people who menstruate'[109] to refer to women, or trans-men, or inter-sex individuals. Sorry, it's hard to keep up with their ever-growing insanity.

In 2022, a local 'Miss America' pageant awarded their crown to an objectively unattractive obese 19-year-old man[110] who goes by Brian. The title comes with bragging rights and a college scholarship[111].

These recent developments in the radical left's war on normalcy have created a new sub-movement: Trans-exclusionary radical feminists, or TERFs[112]. The hateful elites have sown even more division between groups. They split feminists into those who support women and those who support transgenders, and both sides are now at each other's throats. More divide and control tactics succeeding.

Straight people have been attacked verbally, economically, and even physically for years, and the heterophobic hatred is only growing more intense by the day.

When a gay man drove into a crowd at the Fort Lauderdale gay pride parade and killed one person and injured a few others in July of 2021, The Hill[113] enthusiastically reported that anti-LGBT terrorism was responsible for the incident:

"This is a terrorist attack against the LGBT community," [mayor] Trantalis, who was in attendance at the parade, told local station WPLG. "This is exactly what it is. Hardly an accident. It was deliberate, it was premeditated, and it was targeted against a specific person. Luckily they missed that person, but unfortunately, they hit two other people."

The leftist mayor and media propagandists did not bother waiting a moment to learn any details about the incident before blaming straight people for the tragedy. Had they not jumped the gun, they would have learned that the driver was gay and part of the LGBT community and that it was likely nothing more than an accident. Of course, the damage was done, and it is likely that only a tiny fraction of readers saw the small correction in their article that they added after it was initially published and once the frenzy died down. The damage was done by then; millions more Americans believed that this was 'yet another example of straight people being terrorists towards those poor LGBT victims'. That is the exact sort of division that the elites intended to foment.

The elites have propagated animosity between various groups by pushing for young children to be transitioned to the opposite gender. The radical left and the elites are working extremely hard to convince very young kids and toddlers that they are really trapped inside the body of the wrong gender. Children as young as three years old[114] have been transitioned. Family members are being turned against each other. Transgender debates for children make custody battles even more complicated. In the socialist united states, courts have ruled that parents must 'affirm' the gender identity of their children who feel like the opposite gender. A Texas mother contended that her ex-husband should not be allowed to see their son because

They Fear Unity

he does not believe that the boy is really a girl. *"Dr. Georgulas, a pediatrician, had initially petitioned a Dallas court to limit her ex-husband's visits with his children, require that he now refer to James as Luna and keep him away from people who would not "affirm" his gender identity...A Texas jury has ruled against a father seeking to intervene in the gender transition of his seven-year-old son,"* as reported by News.Com.au[115].

As reported by the New York Post: *"Children — as young as 5 — are being encouraged to disregard their anatomy and choose their gender based on their feelings. Last week, a California mother raged*[116] *at the Spreckels Union School District board for allowing teachers to coach her 12-year-old daughter*[117] *on becoming a boy, choosing a boy's name, and hiding the plan from the family."*

When some straight people began to peacefully raise awareness about their own struggle against discrimination, they were predictably mocked[118] and condemned harshly by the mainstream press and Americans at large. The precedent has been set: if you are in the LGBT community, you should be proud and Americans and their elites will celebrate you as a hero on a regular basis. If you are straight, you are a bigoted bastard who should be condemned and shamed incessantly. If you mention 'straight pride', you are as evil as a Nazi, and perhaps you should be killed. If you do not support pediatric transgender fanaticism[119], you are a hateful bigot and a child abuser. That is what many Americans now believe.

While the elites and their blind and rabid followers are determined to make life miserable for 'cis' straight people, many individuals are still not very hateful, though. Most real people (as opposed to full-time leftist activists and Twitter bots) have no animosity toward people for their sexuality. I have no issues with LGBT folks, and they have no issues with me. (As it turns out, a fair amount of my closest friends are gay and/or transgender)

Don't get me wrong: The movement to condemn all straight and 'cis' people as bigots who should be shunned has achieved some success. But the elites need a divider that can apply to 100% of people in the united states. Most people either don't hate others for their sexual preferences or simply don't care what others do in their own bedrooms.

"No...we must keep looking for the perfect way to divide the people!"

Chapter 5: Republicans vs. Democrats

Since George Washington left office in 1797 after two terms as president, the federal government has been controlled by a duopoly; that is, we have always been ruled by two political parties. This is no coincidence, and it's one of the major reasons we have lost so much liberty since Washington. The union's first president actually warned of the dangers of political parties[120] in his farewell address. Unfortunately, this piece of wisdom was completely ignored by the elites who would come into power over the next two centuries, as were his warnings about foreign interventionism[121]. Today, the DC Empire acts as the world police and is run by two parties that pretend to differ from each other just enough to keep each of their constituencies focused on the opposition.

Politicians have always desired to rule by inconspicuous authoritarianism. They understand that allowing for three or more major parties could enable truly competitive elections, which would threaten their permanent stranglehold on power. And they know that one-party rule would be tantamount to a dictatorship, which would be rejected by the people. So, two was the perfect number. Politicians on each side have long acted as if by an unwritten agreement with the other that they would guide the displeasure of their constituents and party members toward the 'opposition' party members and away from the authoritarian government itself. In a one-party system, the disgruntled people focus their anger on the government. In a two-party system, angry Americans can be easily guided to direct their anger at the opposition party. But if leaders of both major parties colluded with each other by agreeing on nearly all major issues while consistently trading personal liberty for government power, the elites would always be safe. It's the perfect plan!

Nearly all politically-aware individuals in the united states believe that the primary issue is that the opposite party is in power or that their opponents have too much influence on the government, even if they don't technically control any of the three branches.

Anarchists (and some libertarians) believe that the primary issue is that the *government* has so much power. They understand that the people who occupy the offices of government are not the primary issue; it's the fact that the government offices wield so much power. Anarchists believe that people should be 100% free and that the government should not exist, while libertarians believe in minimal government.

We have seen this play out countless times in Washington DC, most recently with the omnibus bill[122] of December 2022. A horrible law is passed by Congress. The Republican politicians tell their voters in their fundraising emails to direct all anger at the Democrats and claim that it was all their fault, and that the best way to defeat the Democrats next November is to donate to Republicans. The Democratic politicians do the exact same thing. While everyday voters of both parties use their time, money, and energy trying to 'defeat' the opposition party's elected officials in the next election by donating their hard-earned money or spending their time volunteering for a campaign, the politicians in DC get away with their tyranny unscathed. And they do it together with the 'opposition' party's politicians at the same cocktail parties. Oh, yes - it's just like the WWE; politicians only pretend to hate each other when the cameras are on them. In real life, they are friends with similar values or at least similar goals. And those goals have nothing to do with representing their constituents or protecting our natural individual rights. They are all about power.

Often, the politicians avoid accountability for their actions by passing the buck on major decisions altogether. They allow (and likely encourage) other parts of the government to make the most important decisions so that they can face their constituents with plausible deniability when it comes time to seek their votes for reelection. Congressmen have long had the courts and federal agencies do their dirty work for them. Under Dictator Obama's reign, the 'Environmental Protection Agency' passed[123] nearly 4,000 new "regulations". If you thought that laws (legislation) were supposed to be passed only by the legislative branch (Congress), you were sadly mistaken! Congressmen hardly pass any laws. They raise money for congressional leadership PACs and their party leaders and hope to be rewarded with prestigious committee assignments, party titles, and a small portion of the money when they find themselves in a close election. That's how it really works.

Go ask 100 Republicans who they blame for the most serious problems in the united states. I would bet that at least 80 of them say that the Democrats are the primary problem. And the Democrats would blame the Republicans for nearly all of their troubles. Very few would correctly identify that the *government* is the primary problem. Not the people occupying the offices - but the existence of government. The problem is that we have lords. The names of the lords hardly matter. It does not matter whether they wear red or blue robes. We should not have any lords ruling over us. We should be free to live however we please as long as we don't hurt others. And to those who say that the government's primary duty is to protect those who cannot protect themselves.....well, the government has arguably been doing the exact opposite of protecting people for the past 240 years. Indeed, the government is the biggest threat to our safety, not our greatest protector!

This seemingly minor distinction is of the utmost importance. If the government did not divide Americans into these two camps, the people might all unite and turn their well-warranted frustration on the sociopaths in DC, which would lead to a swift victory for the people and a devastating defeat for the politicians. However, since the elites pretend to fight each other, they are able to successfully convince enough people to hold onto hope that the government could function perfectly and create their utopia if only *their* party could control the entire government. One of the greatest feats accomplished by politicians was convincing their constituents that everything would be perfect if the voters simply gave their party total control over DC. Of course, this would never happen, and politicians are experts at finding scapegoats and excuses, anyway. Republicans claim to support severely diminishing taxes, regulations, gun laws, education controls, and many more authoritarian policies. Yet, they would fail to do so even when given the Presidency, the Supreme Court, and 100% of the seats in the House and Senate. They would claim that it isn't the right time for such radical policy changes, or that people rely on the government for welfare, or that such policies would harm their reelection campaigns, or that they would use a myriad of other excuses. When Republicans had full control over all branches of the federal government in 2017 and 2018, they did practically nothing conservative and perpetuated the progressive socialism that was in place.

Imagine what would happen if there were one-party rule in DC.

Imagine what would happen if all Republicans in the united states gave up all hope of ever reforming the united states government via methods such as 'voting out the Democrats' because they finally realized that Republicans[124] in DC do not support freedom either.

What about the other parties?
There are more than two parties in the united states. The largest of the alternatives is the Libertarian Party, which received 4.5 million votes in the 2016 presidential election. There is also the Green Party, the Constitution Party, and around 100[125] others.

In order to even appear on the election ballot, candidates of a party outside of the duopoly must go door-to-door in their district and get signatures from thousands of voters who believe that the candidate should be allowed to be on the ballot. In order to maintain their minor party status for the next election cycle (generally two years later), the party must receive between two and twenty percent of the popular vote, depending on the state.

Writing for the Independent Political Report[126] in 2022, Richard Manzo explained the arduous process of attaining ballot access in New Hampshire:

"A candidate for Governor or the United States Senate must collect 3,000 certified signatures on nominating papers, each of which may only be signed by a single voter, with 1,500 of those coming from each Congressional district...After collecting at least 3,000 certifiable petitions, along with others that will be rejected for illegibility or bearing a signature of someone not registered to vote, candidates and their volunteers must deliver each signed paper to town and city clerks across the state for the first certification. Some clerks may not understand their responsibility in ensuring nominating papers reach their supervisors of the checklist, but what's universal in each municipality is the completely unnecessary administrative burden imposed on them by obsolete state law...Once the first certification is completed, some municipalities will mail certified nominating papers back to the candidates, and others require personal collection by a candidate or volunteer. Once those are sorted and counted, and a candidate reasonably believes they have enough certified petitions, they're ready to be delivered to

the Secretary of State for a final count and discrepancy check."

Even if these candidates manage to get onto the ballot, they are nearly always excluded from the debates, which are controlled by the duopoly and their cronies in the media. Without the opportunity to debate the Republican and Democrat nominees, there is roughly zero chance a Libertarian could win any major election. The Commission on Presidential Debates[127] is literally run by Democrat and Republican Party leaders. Naturally, it does everything in its power to prohibit outsiders from participating in its debates. In 2016, the CPD told the alternative candidates that they must achieve 15% in polls conducted by ABC/Washington Post, NBC/Wall Street Journal, CBS/New York Times, CNN, or Fox News. They knew that this was an impossible feat, considering that the polls included four candidates and were conducted by pro-duopoly media companies.

So, our rulers will continue to divide people based on party affiliation or other similar characteristics. And the overwhelming majority of sheep will continue to fall for their WWE-style show. The criminals in DC know that they cannot afford to awaken the sleeping giant that is (traditional) American patriotism - the kind displayed by Washington and Jefferson.

Increasingly, Americans are realizing that both major parties are totally out of touch with everyday people, and that party leaders only look out for their own interests. Many Americans identify more as independents than as members of one of the two major parties. Few people vote in primary elections. Only around 28% of eligible voters[128] voted for each major party's presidential candidate in the 2016 general election. This means that nearly 50% of eligible voters decided not to vote for either major party candidate, essentially voting against both. Voter participation in state and local elections is even lower than it is in presidential races.

The dividing aspect of the two-party system has achieved some success, but people are beginning to realize that the DC Empire is run by this duopoly, and voters are growing

If "Did Not Vote" Had Been A Candidate In The 2016 US Presidential Election more frustrated with both parties. Many people are beginning to realize that the Republicans and Democrats in DC are almost indistinguishable from one another.

The elites have realized that even their perfect 'two-party dictatorship' is failing to effectively keep everyone divided and fighting with their neighbors. The search for the perfect divider continues!

This is Ohio. The blue areas are where there are fun and interesting things to do. The red area is where the corn is.

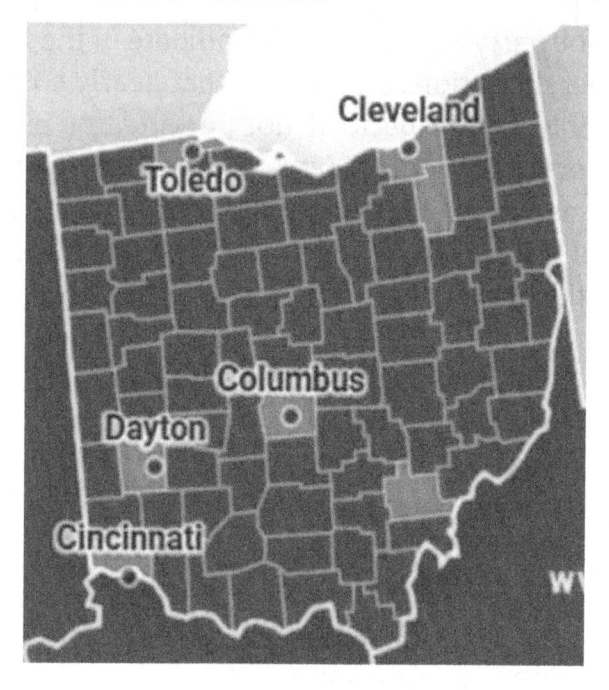

Chapter 6: Corona-Fascism

The latest great divider was implemented as part of the unprecedented onslaught against personal liberties known as 'corona-fascism'.

Since the paranoia surrounding the scamdemic began, individuals throughout the united states began to split into two camps:

1) The first group consisted of people who trusted the elites from DC and their 'experts', who also happened to reside in the capitol and act more like politicians than scientists. These people have been growing increasingly paranoid and anxious about the virus killing them at any moment. They obey the politicians who tell them to wear two masks and get three (or more) vaccines and avoid all human contact indefinitely, despite being at a very low risk of dying from the disease.

2) The second group consisted of people who trusted centuries of science and refused to live in a paranoid and/or authoritarian dystopia. These people largely ignored the scamdemic and/or prioritized personal liberty over absolute safety.

These two diverging groups have been growing apart and continue to do so at the time of this writing. Whenever a new vaccine is approved or a 'booster' is recommended to be taken on a regular basis, the politicians seize the opportunity to drive a wedge between the paranoid corona-fascists and the health freedom advocates.

I regularly hear stories from friends about their siblings, cousins, and acquaintances refusing to be in the same room with them unless they wear the requisite layers of masks or get all the recommended vaccine doses. Countless families and other social groups have been torn apart by corona-fascism, as well. And the elites and their allies in the media are thrilled to stoke the flames of division.

One friend of mine has told me that her family has essentially canceled Christmas and other holidays since 2020. Her relatives refuse to spend time with her unless she caves and gets the jabs. Another friend bought this author's book about corona-fascism[129] and gave it to her sister. When I followed up to ask if her sister enjoyed reading the book, she told me that her sister burned the book. In an actual fire. A corona-fascist burned a gift from her sister because it challenged her cultish beliefs about Lord Fauci and Emperor Biden. There are clearly some powerful forces at play.

Politicians are not just encouraging people to turn on each other, though. Policymakers are literally segregating entire classes of people, and they are doing so based on the premise of corona-fascism.

Jay Inslee, the dictator of Washington State, has mandated that private venues separate and shame[130] those who have not taken the vaccines. *"Under the power of the state, the Inslee administration is encouraging private organizations and religious institutions to create vaccinated-only sections in their venues. Inslee is not merely promoting vaccine segregation; he's even forcing people to use separate entrances when entering venues."*, writes Jason Rantz of MyNorthWest.com.

The tyrants who run NYC have made it illegal[131] for owners of (formerly) private businesses to allow anyone inside unless they show proof of vaccination. This policy will likely spread to other areas of the united states.

Administrators of hospitals and nursing homes are being pressured to fire workers who refuse to receive the sacred vaccine. Those who have high levels of antibodies to COVID are not exempt from this mandate. The horrible shortage of healthcare workers in New Hampshire and throughout the union has not made the elites think twice about their decision to lay off large percentages of medical providers.

In a rare deviation from customer-friendly business practice, store owners began rudely kicking customers out of their stores for the crime of disobeying the latest corona-fascist edicts. This was all due to the policies created by politicians and the pressure exerted on the private establishments by the elites.

One of the many reasons that 'private' businesses are acting as proxy police is that politicians and their cronies have placed immense pressure on the owners to do so. One example involves politicians encouraging private employees to stop working and collect unemployment if their bosses refuse to implement mask and vaccine mandates. This forced the owners to either watch their employees leave work and collect unemployment (why work if you could get paid to sit at home?) or implement the corona-fascist mandates 'voluntarily'. Another example involves courts holding business owners civilly or criminally liable in any case involving a person possibly contracting COVID while at their business - unless the business implemented a mask and vaccine mandate. This obviously incentivizes the business owners to implement the mandates because they can't afford to be held liable in such ridiculous lawsuits. Never mind that it would be impossible to factually prove that a person contracted a specific illness at a specific time and location.

In 2020, the united states acted in lockstep with various other governments to create a massive panic around a virus that was supposedly lingering on every surface, contagious without symptoms, and expected to kill a massive portion of the population. Because of this invisible enemy, our government decided it was prudent to shut down small businesses, quarantine citizens, declare states of emergency everywhere, and suspend our constitutional rights indefinitely.

Our government used "trusted" health authorities, medical "experts", and the "media", to justify these measures and to convince the majority of the population that all of this was necessary to protect public health.

Ironically, the elites pretended that one of their goals was to create unity, with slogans like, *"we're all in this together"*, which became one of the most common phrases used by corona-fascists throughout the scamdemic. But in reality, their goal was to divide us along as many lines as possible.

It started with the introduction of "social distancing" guidelines, which were actually meant to create *physical* distancing. People were conditioned to view all other humans as potential threats, making it easy to convince them that creating an arbitrary 6-foot air gap between themselves and others was a necessary life-saving measure.

Then came the masks, which were initially worn voluntarily by hypochondriacs and germaphobes. The face coverings then became mandatory once hysterics in positions of power felt political pressure to act. Soon, the majority of the population was complying with the orders to wear inappropriate medical devices[132] over their faces during nearly every waking moment, simply because the politicians and their enforcers told them to do so.

Then came the shut-downs, which just meant that all small businesses, churches, gyms, and schools would have to close down indefinitely. At the same time, major corporations and well-connected businesses could remain open because they were deemed "essential" by the politicians.

Although there are many other factors that contributed to corona-fascism, these measures formed the assault on our freedom of assembly. No longer could we freely gather and interact with our neighbors without being subjected to arbitrary rules and unlawful mandates. We were to keep our distance, mask our faces, stay inside, and continue paying our taxes like good patriots (read: sheep).

Not only did this blatantly prove that our constitution could be violated by politicians with impunity, but it made subtle forms of torture acceptable, such as isolation and muzzling. Around half of the members of our society accepted this inhumane treatment, because they have been conditioned to trust people in positions of authority, especially in the medical community.

In reality, these measures, which defied human nature and long-established medical practices, created deep societal divides that may never heal. Preventing us from gathering in person, worshiping God, and running our businesses freely left us with fewer opportunities to find common ground with our neighbors and made it that much harder for the populace to unite against those responsible for fomenting this global health crisis. Planning any sort of resistance to tyranny requires coordination. Savvy individuals understand that nearly all electronic communication could be surveilled by the tyrants. So, they meet in person to coordinate protests, activism, and civil disobedience. Maybe that was why the elites made it so difficult to meet in person during the two-year scamdemic.

As the majority of Americans became brainwashed by peer pressure, unprecedented media campaigns[133], and constant bombardment from every institution in the united states, a new religion came into prominence: the Corona-Cult, also known as the 'Religion of the Mask' or 'Faucism'.

Within a few months, regular citizens were buying into the recommendations of Fauci, Birx, and other narcissistic "leaders". Regular people became paranoid; if you came within 6 feet of them or allowed your mask to slip beneath your nose, they would scold you. Some would even call the police. These reckless COVID-deniers were a danger to public health, after all!

Some politicians even proposed legislation that would make it 'criminal assault' to disobey an order from other civilians[134] who commanded you to put on a mask, maintain a 6-foot distance, or obey any other rule related to corona-fascism.

Religious zealots made a public display of their fidelity to their sacred commandments:

1) Thou shalt wear a mask at all times
2) Hugging and kissing are an abomination unto God
3) Six feet of distance shall be maintained from others at all times

4) All gatherings of people shall be a sin and a desecration to the Lord
5) Upon being exposed to a person with any symptom, thou shalt self-quarantine
6) Thou shalt not seek to work, for the Lord will provide for thee
7) All blame for worldly problems lay at the feet of Trump, for he is the devil
8) Lord Biden is the savior chosen by God Almighty
9) Thou shalt worship healthcare workers; medical experts must be obeyed
10) The word of the Lord shall not be questioned, heresy is condemned by God

Even when totally alone, these devout Covidians wore masks. They took pictures with masks and showed them off on social media and even on their dating profiles. Over the span of a few months, Covidians turned masking into a powerful signal of one's virtue, putting the supposed safety benefits of masking on the back burner. Public health is important, but publicly worshiping God is even more important! Even in video meetings[135], participants were told by politicians to wear masks. Those who did not comply were ostracized.

This new religion[136] spread like wildfire, and quickly became the largest religion in the union. The Religion of the Mask enjoyed widespread adoption all over the world, boasting over a billion believers at its peak. Few people in the world dared to speak out against this religion, for fear of being ostracized or killed[137]. As we often observe when it comes to radical leftist control-freaks, their goals are often regressive in nature. In this case, they successfully regressed the world hundreds of years, all the way back to the age[138] when questioning the church[139] could cost a heretic their life.

Concurrently, other religions were being crushed. More so than a lack of faith, this was due to politicians literally making it a crime to attend church[140] or synagogue[141]. The megalomaniacs were determined to destroy all religions except for their own.

Throughout the disunited states, politicians and their enforcers were prohibiting people from worshiping their Gods by praying in churches. Unlike some laws that are barely enforced, police officers enthusiastically punished Christians and Jews[142] for the crime of praying with others. Church congregations quickly adapted to the new laws, and some churches began to hold prayers in their parking lots, with each person remaining in their own vehicle throughout the service. When cops began to punish these people[143] many worshippers began to realize that corona-fascism was not about safety; it was about control and squashing all other religions.

"*These are really tough decisions.......It would be irresponsible to take anything off the table...*" New Hampshire Governor Sununu solemnly told reporters at a press conference[144] featuring leaders from each part of the state's government.

Less than 24 hours after Sununu issued his order, Liberty Legal PLLC announced a lawsuit[145] against the dictator, seeking to reverse his emergency order that restricted public gatherings and prohibited dining in restaurants. Liberty Legal PLLC filed the lawsuit on behalf of clients Holly Beene, David Binford, and Eric Couture. Attorney Dan Hynes agreed to take the case pro bono, commenting that "*it is an important constitutional issue.*"

An outspoken conservative and former State Representative, Hynes has not been shy about his disagreement with the dictator's order. The attorney and his clients believe that the executive order violates the Constitution, our natural freedoms, and will hurt the economy, according to their lawsuit. Further, the dictator's mandate that police "enforce" his order is vague, overly broad, and lacks legal authority.

A New Hampshire judge denied the plaintiffs' motion for an immediate injunction to halt the order. According to the court, laws that prohibit gathering do not violate the constitution.

On May 8th, 2020, The Louisville Courier-Journal[146] reported that a federal judge overturned a previous ruling banning in-person worship in Kentucky. The judge ruled that Governor Beshear could not prohibit the act of attending church while still allowing people to gather in supermarkets, work meetings, and the governor's press meetings. Many conservatives and libertarians see this ruling as a win for freedom of religion. Here's why I think that this ruling is terrible for the cause of liberty.

In the face of tyranny, we often hear from self-proclaimed conservatives and constitutional scholars that *"...we have constitutional rights, damn it! And no politician can take those rights away!"* In my more naive days, I, too, made such statements. But aren't these statements inherently self-contradictory? On one hand, conservatives profess that rights cannot be taken away by any man (politician, lawyer, judge, voter, etc.). On the other hand, conservatives believe that once a vote occurs or a court ruling is issued, it becomes law – and *"you gotta follow the law, no matter what!"*, as we are often reminded by 'constitutional conservatives'.

In this specific case, Kentucky's new leftist dictator made it a crime[147] to attend church services. He even instructed his armed enforcers to punish people[148] for attending 'drive-in' services and praying in their vehicles, for some unknown reason.

"Two other federal judges in Kentucky — David Hale of Louisville and William Bertelsman of Covington — had previously ruled that the ban on in-person church services was constitutional", the Journal reported. Another federal judge later ruled that the ban on praying in church was

unconstitutional and could not be enforced. Thanks to this judge, Kentuckians are now free to exercise their natural rights to assembly, expression, and religion once more. Should they be grateful to this government official for 'giving' them the right to pray? Should they worry about whether the next judge to rule on this case decides that Beshear's order was constitutional? How could they possibly pray in peace under such circumstances?

This is what we should expect to occur when we leave our natural (not constitutional – but natural) rights to be interpreted and controlled by sociopathic judges and politicians. What would God say if you told him that you would not worship him properly because a politician or a judge 'ruled' that it's illegal to do so? Do you serve God or do you serve the government? Do you remember God's second commandment? I'll give you a hint: it does not allow you to worship your government over your God.

We have seen a very similar phenomenon occur with the 2nd amendment. Each politician and judge 'interprets' the natural right in their own way, and all 340,000,000 individuals throughout the union must give up their firearms and accessories or change their habits with each new court decision[149] or ATF[150] ruling. As with so many other issues, every June we wait with bated breath to find out what our Constitution says - according to the Supreme Court. If our right to bear arms is natural and inalienable, let's make that known to our elected officials and judges. If the right to exercise our religion is natural and inalienable, let's stop waiting for judges and politicians to 'allow' us to pray. Many of us believe that the 1st amendment is already severely limited[151] and that freedom of speech, press, and religion no longer exist in the united states except when explicitly granted to an individual by the government.

As long as we cheer such court rulings as 'great wins' for liberty and conservatism, we will forever remain in the subservient position to the organized criminals[152] who call themselves 'government'. Politicians, lawyers, judges, and voters cannot 'give' us any rights, because our rights belong to each of us as individuals. Your rights to free speech, religion, property, and self-defense are yours and only yours. Nobody can give them to you, nor can they rightfully take them from you. If a judge ruled that you were allowed to breathe, you would not thank him. You would condemn him for having the audacity to believe that such a right was his to give. Why should other natural rights be any different?

The corona-fascists in the government, media, and popular culture are successfully making anyone who does not submit to the Cult of Corona into second-class citizens.

"This divider is working quite well, but could we continue to use a 'state of emergency' based on a virus forever? Let's keep searching for the ultimate divider!"

They Fear Unity

♡ ○ ▽   ⊓

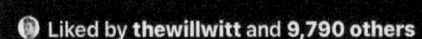

🌐 Liked by **thewillwitt** and **9,790 others**

ginajcarano A current events picture of a grocery store in Germany separating the vaxed from the unvaxxed.
When will you draw your line?
When will you speak up? When will enough be enough?
When this comes to a grocery store near you and someone you love is on the other side?
What side of history do you really think you're on if you complied and encouraged this.
It...has... gone... WAY...too... far.... Do not be a part of it. For humanity and for future generations.
#DoNOTComply has everything to do with each individual personal choice. Let's make sure these mandates are lifted and stay that way. 🙏

Chapter 7: The Ultimate Divider

Leftist politicians and activists have seemingly settled on 'toxic masculinity' for their latest attempt to divide their serfs. Actually, it is hardly a new concept. In fact, it meshes quite well with the radical progressive agenda that is increasingly referred to as the 'femi-nazi' movement, which has essentially established a stranglehold on the entire Democratic party and progressive movement, and nearly all of 'feminism'. Radical leftist feminism focuses on villainizing males at every single opportunity. The left now seems to believe that being male is enough reason to consider a person evil. Males are all guilty by default.

The plan is simple and it fulfills two of their critical criteria at once:

1) Turn (up to) 100% of Americans against each other based on gender warfare.

2) Destroy the nuclear family, creating a void for the almighty government to fill.

Will it work?

This new, super-radical brand of misandrist feminism has spread throughout the political class and Hollywood, augmented by the recent 'Me Too' movement. Many women and some men throughout the united states have seemingly accepted 'toxic masculinity' as a legitimate concept. Perhaps more importantly, many large companies have jumped onto the anti-male bandwagon, likely in an effort to appear 'woke' or pro-social-justice to potential consumers and/or to ensure that the radical leftist mob spares them when they seek to destroy all major companies that do not engage in their radical activism. Gillette was one of the many companies to join the movement, and the response to their video ad[153] painting men as sexual predators has been overwhelmingly negative, thankfully. Only time will tell how successful the left's mission to persecute men will be. Fortunately, many parents will continue to teach their children that it is not a crime to be male....at least until being male literally becomes illegal.

Bait and pushback
Of course, another way of looking at this well-thought-out effort is that it could be bait. The radical left may be intentionally pushing so hard against men in order to make men

defensive and make themselves appear foolish, radical, or "hyper-masculine". If this is the short-term goal of the movement, it is a very simple and easy one to achieve. All they need to do is continue calling men reckless, evil predators. When men become defensive and claim that they are not reckless and violent, they can respond with a 'GOTCHA!' by proving that men are statistically responsible for nearly all violent crimes and that men are by nature more reckless.

Utilization of half-truths
This brings us to perhaps the most significant reason that this divider is so successful. It is based on scientific facts; men are, by their very nature, more aggressive and reckless. I don't deny this fact, and few men would. The divisive elites take this genetic fact – one which men cannot change – and they take it a dangerous step further. The movement asserts that men are naturally more aggressive, and therefore, we are all EVIL. Because the movement's message does begin with a truth, it is understandable how some naive onlookers could fall for it. What the feminazis don't mention is that all individuals in society (women included) benefit from men having the genetic characteristics[154] bequeathed upon them

by their creator. The majority of military personnel in combat roles are male. Males represent nearly all hard labor and protection services. Males are biologically required in order to have children, so, simply put, the human race would go extinct in one generation without males. This may seem obvious to some, but it seems that ultra-radical feminists[155] get so wrapped up in their hatred for men that they forget how much they really do need men in order for their species to survive.

Hypocrisy
As we touched upon earlier, the entire message of the feminist movement is based on hypocrisy: 'men are horrible creatures who should be shamed, sanctioned[156], and violently punished'[157]. At the same time, the leftist feminist message is that there are literally no differences[158] between men and women. Linear logic would conclude that women are evil if they are identical to men and if men are evil. But the elite dividers have little regard for logic. In fact, logic is condemned as bigoted and non-woke. Additional hypocrisy within this ridiculous movement involves companies lecturing men about objectifying women while simultaneously objectifying women to help market their products to men (sex sells, even when utilized

by self-proclaimed socialist feminists). Additionally, if hateful feminist companies really support 'equality', they must also begin lecturing women on 'toxic femininity', wherein women murder babies, smoke and drink while pregnant, make up false rape allegations, coerce boys to commit suicide, etc. If Gillette and other leftist companies do not produce such a video, they are not in favor of equality, they are just hateful and sexist towards men.

Title IX
In 1972, President Nixon signed legislation called the 'Education Amendments of 1972'[159]. Title IX of the law read that:

"No person in the United States shall, based on sex, be excluded from participation in, be denied the benefits of, or be subjected to discrimination under any education program or activity receiving Federal financial assistance."

This applies to nearly every college and university in the united states. As of 2017, all but 18 colleges[160] in the union accepted federal money. Title IX seems like a relatively simple law. It was clearly intended to prevent outright discrimination, such as colleges banning women or preventing them from taking math classes. But politicians and college administrators have used the law to impose their dystopian desires on college students throughout the union. By granting women similar privileges to their male counterparts in athletics, they caused great harm to their male athletes.

Politicians and college administrators have decided that if a college's student body is 50% male and 50% female, its athletics programs must also be 50% male and 50% female. If only 38 females in the whole school want to play any sport while 3,000 males want to play sports, it doesn't matter. If the football team happens to be national champions who also happen to bring the school more revenue and prestige than all other sports teams combined, the men must still be punished. The women must have the same status as the men. Such a premise is akin to the NBA being forced by politicians to match its players' racial and gender breakdown to the racial and gender breakdown of the entire united states population. If you don't believe that the NBA should be legally compelled to be exactly 50% female, 52% White, 19% Hispanic, and 6% Asian, then you should oppose Title IX as it is applied.

Another terrible result of Title IX is the dystopian judicial system that it created for sexual crime accusations within the college world.

Since the tragic Duke lacrosse case[161], which should have been a cautionary tale for opponents of due process, not much has changed. In fact, justice and the feminist-induced gender war on college campuses have continued to worsen.

In 2011, President Obama threatened to pull federal funding from any college that did not investigate and adjudicate all accusations of sexual assault. Predictably, this scared colleges into treating sexual assault *accusations* almost as *convictions* and swiftly punishing the accused before due process could take its course. Fearful of losing their precious federal funding, colleges invested large amounts of money and resources in their semi-governmental independent justice systems, complete with 'Title IX Officers', hearings, and punishments.

When a male student is accused of sexual assault, for instance, college administrators presume the suspect to be guilty and punish him, often before due process occurs. The same goes for professors accused of sexual misconduct for offending students by committing heinous sex crimes, such as writing controversial articles[162], singing Beach Boys[163] songs, or giving a female student a B+ as a final grade[164].

In 2014, a federal appeals court ruled that a high school boys' basketball coach violated Title IX when he required his players to have short hair[165]. This was considered 'discrimination' because the girls who played basketball on the female team were allowed to have long hair. Remember, *"there shall be no difference between males and females, so sayeth the Lord!"*

The law has also been used to expand and distort the complex world of sex crimes.

What does discrimination have to do with sex crimes?

Well, if women believe that females are raped on a daily basis in college, they will have a horrible educational experience, of course. Because men do not have the same problem, this means that women are being discriminated against, because they are inherently more likely to have a negative college experience due to the irrational but technically factual fear that they are more likely to be raped than their male counterparts. This would be the equivalent of designating the Bronx as legally discriminatory because White people are emotionally harmed by the fear that they are more likely to be assaulted in the Tremont neighborhood of the Bronx than their Black and Hispanic counterparts. So, the radicals began to use Title IX for sexual assault. And that's when things really began to spiral out of control.

Over the next few decades, a few SCOTUS rulings allowed the misandrists to expand the law as they desired. In 1992, the SCOTUS ruled in Franklin v. Gwinnett County Public Schools[166] that harassment potentially *"denies its victims the equal access to education that Title IX is designed to protect"*.

The SCOTUS has a reputation for blowing matters way out of proportion and expanding laws to mean things that they clearly were never intended to mean. It often seems to err on the side of authoritarianism and against freedom and due process. This case is a classic example of such judicial tyranny. By the same exact logic, Walmart, the town hall, and every institution in the united states could be sued under the exact same premise: women are more likely than men to be sexually harassed, so they are inherent victims of discrimination due to their perpetual anxiety related to this fact. Why shouldn't women sue CVS? I'm sure that females are more likely than males to be sexually assaulted inside CVS pharmacies. This means that CVS is essentially 'discriminating' against women by 'denying them equal access to the public accommodations of their pharmacy'. Technically, women in all areas of this planet are more likely than their male counterparts to be sexually assaulted. Using the logic endorsed by the highest court in the united states, this means that women are discriminated against due to being put in fear more than men, which makes every entity on the planet guilty of discrimination. Of course, anyone with more than a dozen brain cells could imagine how astronomically preposterous this line of thinking could become; by the same metric, all people in the world are potential victims of discrimination. I feel afraid when I go outside. And the statistics[167] back up my fears. Where's my compensation?

All of these issues cause increasing resentment between the sexes. Males feel attacked by college administrators, politicians, and their female counterparts. Women feel afraid of being attacked by men due to the constant propaganda painting men as violent savages. Many believe that Title IX was one of the most divisive laws ever passed. This divider is working quite well. In the 2022 elections, exit polls found that 70% of single women[168] voted Democrat. It is clear that the elites have successfully convinced many women that men are their enemies, and that only Democrats can protect them.

Yet, it seems that the ambitious leftist elites will not be satisfied until they find the perfect way to turn people against each other.

> This woman is the Deputy Editor of Huffington Post! If someone tweeted this about women it would IMMEDIATELY be a police matter!
>
> **Emily McCombs** ✓
> @msemilymccombs
>
> New Year's resolutions:
> 1. Cultivate female friendships
> 2. Band together to kill all men
>
> 12:54 PM · 1/2/23
>
> 8.8K   1.3K

Chapter 8: The War On Family, Religion, & Gathering

Traditional families have formed the foundation of cohesive societies for as long as civilization has existed. However, the radical left generally views this tradition as a threat to their version of "progress". Instead of recognizing the value of the family unit, they are hellbent on destroying the concept altogether. They may claim that it is part of their effort to be more 'inclusive' of other methods of organization that individuals may choose. But many believe that their real motive is to supplant the family with the government.

Of course, exceptions to the traditional nuclear family exist, but in order to live fulfilling and prosperous lives, we need to agree on certain standards for our children. Unfortunately, this means that some people will be pushed to the "fringe" and will live outside of the generally accepted standards. The left can't accept these inherent differences because they believe that all people are literally equal and that everyone is capable and deserving of the exact same outcomes in life.

For the left, "leveling the playing field" means pretending that differences don't exist and attempting to normalize fringe values by promoting late-term abortions, alternative lifestyles, promiscuity, and single motherhood, all so the outliers don't feel that they are any different. At the same time, they condemn 'standard' heterosexual couples with children.

None of this changes the fact that the nuclear family is the ideal. We can pretend that it's not true, but it is undeniable that children are better off when their biological parents stay together to raise them. Naming exceptions to rules does not change this truth.

When many whole families live in close proximity to one another, they make up the safe and high-trust communities that so many people consider to be desirable. These communities don't magically appear due to coincidence, good luck, the government, or White privilege. They're formed by like-minded, family-oriented, and often religious or spiritual people. Members of these communities are far from perfect, but their communities still serve as a model for a society that functions in a way that many people desire.

The leftist politicians and activists twist this model into some form of unachievable perfection meant to exclude the "other", but this familial ideal is not about being perfect, it's about accountability and responsibility to others. All families know hardship and strife, but the time and dedication people give to one another distinguishes loving families from dysfunctional ones.

When people value *people* over material and superficial things, their spirituality manifests itself in the form of community and unity. This familial unity offends the radical left because they know that it excludes the dysfunctional. They blame it on hate, homophobia, racism, and White privilege, which are all excuses to coddle the outsider and to affirm their deviant values.

The leftist utopia is not a unified place where differences are simply acknowledged. No, their dream is of a diversified hellhole where people are required to pretend that it is possible to be both different and identical at the same time.

The bottom line is that family *is*, by its very nature, exclusive. It's not meant to hurt feelings or to make others feel bad about their dispositions in life. Traditional families exist for the purpose of rearing children; to perpetuate the human race in a civilized, safe, and productive manner. This is not to condemn non-traditional families or outsiders. There's a place for everyone, but a strong society must unite around certain basic norms if it hopes to be safe and prosperous.

The united states were founded on Judeo-Christian ideals. By no means does that mean that all persons throughout the union must be devout Jews or Christians (this author is agnostic). But it does require them to acknowledge that they were born into this world with inherent natural rights, which cannot be granted or eliminated by fellow mortals.

For the God-fearing, this is where the church comes in. The church is a place to unite with like-minded people to give thanks and praise to the creator for his grace. It's a place where individuals unite around common beliefs and values that they intend to pass down to their descendants.

There are several reasons why this is threatening to the authoritarian elites. First, because the church defines good and righteous living. Second, because the church creates barriers to temptations. Third, because having faith in a creator frees believers from the bondage of worshiping other men, which is what the authoritarians often rely on to coerce us to bend to their will. (See: the blind worship of Barack Obama, George Bush, Hillary Clinton, Joe Biden, Anthony Fauci, Donald Trump, etc.)

The radical left responds to these threats through destruction, not with fire and brimstone, but with subversion. New, more 'inclusive' forms have emerged along with new, less offensive versions of the Bible. Add in anti-liberty pastors and a progressive pope, and before long, the word of God is so watered down that it is essentially meaningless.

A union of people who respect western values means that citizens are *united* by agreeing on a basic set of morals. This is what determines our customs and how we deal with each other as a society. Leftists think these are simply socially constructed standards set in place by racist colonizers to create barriers to their 'anything goes' culture. So, their war on religion and families persists through destruction, division, and subversion, and you can be sure that strength and unity are not their end goals.

Instead of working toward maintaining the founding principles, we're now forced to accept a multitude of standards to show how progressive and virtuous we all are.

We're told that diversity is truly a strength and that if we accept it, we can progress to a culturally superior society. However, destroying faith and family at the same time is no way to achieve growth. In the absence of a common value system, we end up with a nation of rampant consumerism, depravity, and materialism.

If we allow the war on western religion, family, and morality to continue, we will further erode the diminishing unity within the united states. When unity is absent, a low-trust society will take hold and the only way to manage such a society that has lost its ties to morality is through brute force, coercion, and violence. And a powerful central government will happily fill that void once institutions such as families and religious communities dissolve. This is what's in store for us if the left's war is not stopped in its tracks.

For decades, the radical left has made it clear that the destruction of the nuclear family unit was one of their primary goals. Ever since the federal government began to subsidize and encourage single motherhood[169], the rates of fatherless children[170] began to climb. Socialist President Lyndon Johnson's 'war on poverty' did not decrease poverty. Much like the 'war on drugs', it failed to reduce the prevalence, made matters worse[171], and forced people like you and me to fund all the failed policies.

Since the massive new welfare programs were created by politicians in 1964 (and expanded many times since), single-parent birth rates have steadily increased, as demonstrated by the chart below:

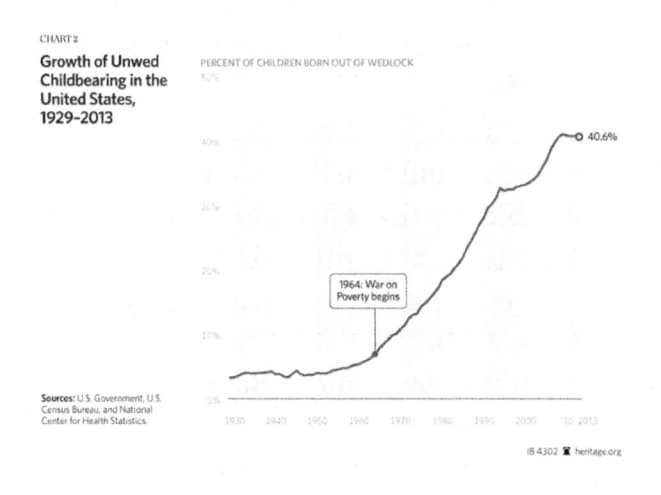

CHART 2

Growth of Unwed Childbearing in the United States, 1929-2013

PERCENT OF CHILDREN BORN OUT OF WEDLOCK

40.6%

1964: War on Poverty begins

Sources: U.S. Government, U.S. Census Bureau, and National Center for Health Statistics.

IB 4302 heritage.org

Concurrently, the radical left has been waging war against Judeo-Christian religions and values. From Obama using the IRS to target Christian non-profits[172], to the massive campaigns against Christian businesses[173] and churches and all the media and boycotts in between, it is common knowledge that progressives hate religious people. Indeed, much of their platform flies in the face of Judeo-Christian values.

Leftists are anti-life, believe in a disturbingly radical LGBT agenda, support theft, violate the second commandment regularly (Thou shalt have no other gods before me), and are hateful sinners of the highest degree. The few leftists who claim to be religious Christians are seemingly hypocrites, who violate biblical laws daily (, premarital sex, abortion, unwarranted hatred, theft, etc.).

An entire book could easily be (and probably has been) written on the left's war against families and religious communities. The bottom line is that the communist doctrine requires all institutions to be abolished and replaced with an omnipotent government. So, the family unit, churches, and other groups must be extinguished before the government can be omnipotent, which is the new left's goal. Make no mistake; Democrats - and quite possibly the majority of Americans - want the government to have unlimited power and individual people to have no freedom to do anything without government permission.

Of course, the war against religion, families, and gatherings was going very well for the tyrants. But corona-fascism gave their efforts a huge boost. A new battle began in 2020, which exacerbated the war on religion and family, and it's still ongoing as of this writing. This is the battle against our freedom of association by way of medical tyranny. If the elites win this battle, it is the final nail in the coffin for human freedom.

As we learned during corona-fascism, assembly became all but illegal due to the lockdowns. The elites surely know that humans communicate most effectively in person. Think about your last meeting with someone that was face-to-face. It was most likely pleasant and communication was likely very clear. Compare that interaction to your last virtual conversation via text or online. Of course, the likelihood of miscommunication and hostility is far greater when the two individuals are not physically in the same location. The less real-life interaction people have with one another, the harder it is for them to work together in a united way to oppose a tyrannical government.

In 2020, a judge in New Hampshire determined that lockdowns prohibiting assembly[174] do not violate the natural right to assembly. Never mind that this natural right is clearly protected by the constitution.

All of these efforts have caused many people to fight over religious and family values. The elites have successfully induced atheists to hate Jews, Muslims to despise Christians, gay couples to resent straight couples, and so on. This division has been relatively successful for the tyrants, and it has helped them avoid a united onslaught by the populace to take back their liberties from the politicians. However, many people reject this attempt at division and continue to love one another. Religion in the united states continues to decline as people become increasingly secular and liberal, but other non-governmental institutions are filling the void. Thus, the elites must continue to find ways to divide and control us.

Chapter 9: Generational Hatred

An interesting form of division began to gain popularity recently. Likely due to strong support from the elites, intergenerational strife has grown quite a bit over the past few decades.

As you have likely noticed, young adults often disparage their elders as 'stupid boomers'[175] and blame them for creating the terrible economic[176] and cultural situation that now plagues the union. Some young people are primarily upset that the prior generation allowed the politicians to grow the government so drastically while indebting future generations with incalculable burdens. Others believe that the elder generation is responsible for racism, global warming, and economic inequality. Many young individuals believe that old people got us into the endless and futile wars[177] that are being waged all over the world. There is little dispute that young people currently have a lot of resentment toward their seniors.

Likewise, elderly people often criticize younger generations, claiming that they are lazy and entitled brats who need 'safe spaces' whenever they are offended.

"Get a job and quit your whining! I worked over 40 hours a week since I was 15 and paid for my own college!"

"Shut up, old man! I am already $30,000 in debt from college, and I need to go back for a master's degree if I want to get a decent job, and there is no way I'll ever be able to afford to live in this terrible economy that you old people created!"

We have all heard these types of exchanges between old and young individuals many times.

Which person is right? Are old people responsible for the devaluation of the dollar and college degrees? Are young people entitled losers who are experts at 'being offended' but imbeciles when it comes to everything else?

I think that many people in every generation could bear some of the blame, but that is not necessarily the important part.

The focal point here is the concept of 'divide and conquer'. If the old people believe that young people are their primary opposition, and if young people believe that those seniors are the cause of their problems, both groups will fail to see that politicians, their enforcers, and their enablers are the ones who actually violate our natural rights and do the greatest harm to our lives.

In June 2020, a leftist propaganda site published an article that fanned the flames of the intergenerational wars. The article titled "So Gen Z-ers hate millennials now? A handy guide to the generation wars"[178] sought to foment even more hatred between the five living generations.

Interestingly, Democratic congressional candidates won among 67% of voters ages 18 to 29 in 2018. This represented a greater than **2-to-1 margin** over the 32% of young people who voted for Republicans, as reported by USA Today[179].

Less than three months before the 2022 elections, President Biden announced[180] that the Democrat-controlled federal government would be 'forgiving' up to $20,000 of debt for students who borrowed money from the federal government. Of course, the President does not have the authority to unilaterally pass laws - only Congress has legislative authority. The Democrats knew that this would likely be struck down by federal courts, due to being unconstitutional as per article 1 of the US Constitution. But the elites knew that the courts could not stop his loan-forgiveness policy before many Democrats cast their votes (bearing in mind that millions of Democrats vote weeks before election day since corona-fascism made them fear voting in person and that early, no excuse, mail-in voting with is increasingly permitted throughout the union).

The basic rules of mathematics, logic, and economics state that all debts are paid, either by the borrower or the lender. If a debtor doesn't repay their loan, it means the person who lent them the money is losing that money - meaning that he pays for it. In the case of the federal government, this means that American taxpayers are paying for the college loans. Practically speaking, the federal government is much more likely to print the money than it is to increase taxes to fund the hundreds of billions in loan forgiveness. And printing money causes each dollar in circulation to lose its value, which means that dollar-holders can buy less with their fiat currency than they could previously. Practically speaking, this means that they have become poorer. Thus, inflation is a tax on everyone who holds dollars, because all dollar-holders are losing real value each time the DC elites print billions more dollars. Maybe this is why so many people are exchanging their dollars for alternative currencies like silver, gold, and various cryptocurrencies.

This brilliant ploy of loan forgiveness can foster multiple types of division. It can cause those without outstanding federal student debt to resent the people they are being forced to bail out. It can cause the less educated people to resent the college-educated people who already earn nearly double[181] as much as they do. But most importantly, this is likely to cause older people who either skipped college, paid as they went, or paid off their loans in full to resent these spoiled younger brats.

A federal judge blocked Biden's executive order, but not until two days after election day[182]. Those with student loans will not have their debt forgiven (as of this writing), and they were played[183] by the Democrats like fiddles, yet again.

Despite achieving some degree of success, power-hungry elites have realized that a generational war would not be effective enough. The fact remains - at least for now - that too many people still love or respect their elders. People love their parents and grandparents. Homeowners care about their elderly neighbors. Seniors adore their grandchildren. In many communities, especially religious ones, young children are still taught to respect their elders with immense honor. Growing up, there were certain things I simply would not fathom doing or saying in front of an older person. I still feel obligated to give up my seat for an older person if the elder is standing. Until the radical leftists can totally eliminate the concept of families (and they are trying to do just that - and are seeing great success), this will not be the best way to divide and control the people.

"No.....we must go back to the drawing board!"

Chapter 10: Enviro-Fascism vs. Humanity

Over the past few decades, the socialists who control the DC Empire have made it clear that they despise humanity. At first, this concept may be difficult for some to comprehend; how could humans hate humanity? Wouldn't this make all progressives suicidal? Not exactly. But maybe.

The idea that humans are not the highest life form on Earth is a tenet of Modern Cultural Marxism. If humans are paramount, then human rights may be considered paramount. And as we know, tyrants can dominate the populace only at the expense of human rights. Thus, human rights and humanity itself must be diminished in order for an authoritarian government to flourish.

Enter: Radical Environmentalism, also known as 'Enviro-Fascism'.

As leftists grew their 'Green Revolution' by selling it as the movement for 'clean air', 'clean water', and by utilizing other

> **THINK**
> Opinion, Analysis, Essays
>
> THOUGHT EXPERIMENT
> Science proves kids are bad for Earth. Morality suggests we stop having them.
>
> We need to stop pretending kids don't have environmental and ethical consequences.

nebulous (but effective) maxims as propaganda, they captured large populations and brainwashed them into their cult. In 2006, a former Democratic Senator, Vice President, and twice-failed presidential candidate created a documentary that changed the political landscape and fomented massive amounts of tyranny through division. Al Gore's movie, titled *'An Inconvenient Truth'*, argued that the world was rapidly warming, that it was caused by industrious humans, and that the warming would be catastrophic and irreversible within a few years. Possibly in a longshot attempt to eclipse his insane claim that he invented the internet[184], Gore promised in 2006 that Manhattan would be underwater[185] within 20 years. He has made many other ridiculous predictions and guarantees, including that there is *"a 75 percent chance the entire polar ice cap will melt[186] in summer within the next five to seven years."*

In reality, the amount of polar ice is increasing, according to NASA[187], a division of the progressive federal government. And the island of Manhattan remains as dry as Gore's airplanes[188] and beach-front properties[189].

His 2006 movie generated $24 million in the united states and another $26 million abroad. His numerous books about global warming and his many celebrity endeavors have earned him millions more in profits. His net worth is now estimated at over $300 million[190]. He has clearly benefited immensely from the hoax that he played a major role in proliferating.

The progressive left followed Gore's lead and began moving full steam ahead on global warming hysteria. Of course, they mostly packaged it as 'environmentalism'. It is impossible for anyone to oppose 'protecting the environment' or 'ensuring that air and water are clean'. It's much harder to sell 'global warming' to the masses, especially when you're just recovering from a horrible attempt at pushing 'global cooling'[191] alarmism; insisting that the world was entering an ice age that would destroy the Earth by the year 2000. This movement created thousands of environmental activists who still engage in political activism today. These enviro-fascists often advocate for policies they truly believe in, misguided[192] as they may be.

Greenpeace, a leading progressive enviro-fascist group, condemns the logging of trees, writing on their website[193] that *"...ending deforestation is our best chance to conserve wildlife and defend the rights of forest communities. On top of that, it's one of the quickest and most cost-effective ways to curb global warming. That's why we're campaigning for a deforestation-free future."* The folks at Greenpeace and others in the enviro-fascist movement believe that any human who supports cutting down any trees is evil and must be eradicated. Consequently, those who benefit from logging often believe that enviro-fascists are malicious or mentally unstable individuals with whom they cannot peacefully coexist.

Of course, logging is environmentally beneficial and allows trees to grow back[194] in a healthy cycle, often quite quickly. The alternative is to allow trees to grow unrestricted, causing all sorts of environmental issues, including the many forest fires[195] plaguing California and the northwest of the union over the past few years. Additionally, cutting trees is necessary in order to produce wood, which is used in billions of everyday products throughout the world. Anyone who has ever used anything containing wood, cardboard, or paper should thank a logger. In 2018, American loggers produced over 18 million tons[196] (that's 36 billion pounds) of wood, according to the EPA. This wood is used to make products we all use daily, from paper items to cardboard and kitchen tables. Additionally, we recycle over 3 million tons and combust over 2 million tons for energy production each year. As capitalists, loggers and forestry economists[197] are very concerned with efficiency, because it translates to more money, less work, and a cleaner and more sustainable environment for everyone.

Enviro-fascists opposed paper and cardboard products for the same reason, so they forced governments to outlaw wood products and compel everyone to use plastic for everyday items like grocery bags. They then protested against plastic due to its petroleum (oil) content and its negative effects on sea life when not disposed of properly.

As of this writing, plastic is being banned by local governments all over the union. The misguided enviro-fascists are now forcing people to switch back to paper products for everything from shopping bags to drinking straws. The war on plastic is in full effect, and now the war on paper is losing steam among the radical progressives. But they still hate paper products. I know, it's all very confusing. They seem to want all paper and all plastic banned.

In 2014, California politicians[198] banned disposable plastic bags and forced stores to charge a 10-cent fee for recycled paper bags, reusable plastic bags, and compostable bags. These progressives are punishing people for using recycled and compostable products. Some of us can remember when environmentalists supported recycling and composting! Some believe that California should literally ban every material in existence in order to keep things simple. The socialist, enviro-fascist state already has a law that forces nearly all businesses that are located in the state or that might ship products into the state to warn customers with labels on essentially all foods and products[199] saying that they technically could contribute to cancer. This literally includes lamps, amusement parks, and nearly anything that is edible. In many areas, we have gone full circle and back to paper bags. In 2023, England banned[200] single-use plastic cups, cutlery, and other plastic items. The country only accounts for 0.05% of the world's mismanaged waste, so it won't make much of a difference to the world's oceans. New Jersey

They Fear Unity

also banned all 'single-use' bags[201], including both paper and plastic. But legislators in the Marxist state are now considering repealing the ban[202] on paper bags because their constituents are having trouble carrying all of their groceries with their bare hands.

Over the past few years, hundreds of cities[203] throughout the union have banned plastic bags. This seemingly means that it is now a crime to distribute and/or possess plastic bags in those cities. Other municipalities have begun to require a fee or tax on every single plastic bag used by consumers at checkout. Many cities have also begun to ban plastic straws[204], often beginning by making it a crime for restaurant employees to offer a plastic straw to a customer. Democratic lawmakers[205] in my state recently proposed a bill to criminalize offering plastic straws [206] to customers and another bill that would make it a crime for cashiers to offer plastic or paper bags[207] to customers. The argument used by enviro-fascist radicals in favor of banning plastic generally involves the theory that the majority of plastic is used once, thrown on the street, and makes its way into our oceans, causing terrible harm to marine life and to the Earth.

Just how much plastic is mismanaged, though? And is plastic disposal improving around the world or is the problem worsening? And are Americans the greatest polluters?

According to OurWorldInData.org[208], the percentage of global plastic waste being recycled or incinerated is increasing dramatically each year, while the amount discarded is decreasing each year. In 1980, zero plastic was recycled or incinerated. In the year 2000, 9% of the Earth's plastic waste was recycled, 15% was incinerated, and 76% was thrown in the trash. In 2015, 19.5% of the plastic waste in the world was recycled, 25.5% was incinerated, and 55% was discarded. The graphic below, found on the aforementioned website, shows this incredibly environmentally friendly trend throughout the world.

So, why are progressives attacking plastic now more than ever before? They should be getting happier, not angrier, right?

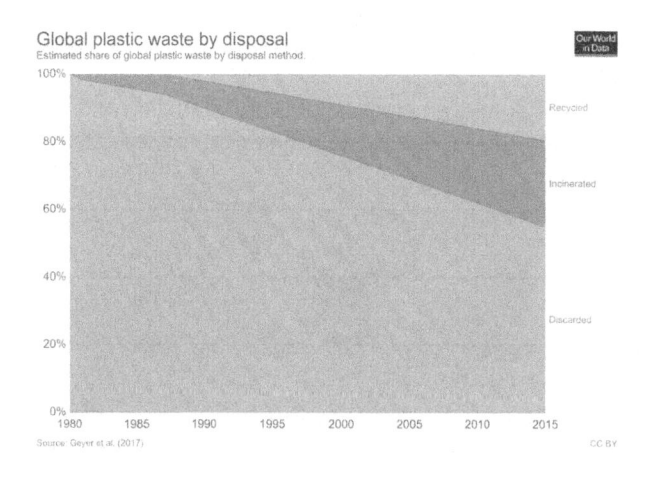

Global plastic waste by disposal
Estimated share of global plastic waste by disposal method.

[Chart showing Recycled, Incinerated, and Discarded shares from 1980 to 2015. Source: Geyer et al. (2017)]

The site also provides statistics on what percentages of plastic waste each country mismanages. As the graphic below demonstrates, China mismanages 74% of its plastic waste, and 4 other nations mismanage at least 50% of their plastic waste. Individuals in the united states mismanage an estimated 0% of their plastic waste. Once littering is factored into the equation, the union accounts for less than 1% of the Earth's mismanaged plastic waste, according to the data. Littering is already a crime, so additional laws would theoretically do little to decrease this issue, anyway.

Share of plastic waste that is inadequately managed, 2010

Share of total plastic waste that is inadequately managed. Inadequately disposed waste is not formally managed and includes disposal in dumps or open, uncontrolled landfills, where it is not fully contained. Inadequately managed waste has high risk of polluting rivers and oceans. This does not include 'littered' plastic waste, which is approximately 2% of total waste (including high-income countries).

Source: Jambeck et al. (2015)

According to another source[209], the entire union and Europe combine to account for only 2% of the oceans' plastic waste. Asia accounts for 82% of the oceans' plastic waste, though. Shouldn't enviro-fascist politicians and activists be condemning Asian countries and praising Americans for being the most environmental consumers on Earth?

Many more sources confirm this data, and Liberty Block contributor Michael Sennello recently explained the data very clearly by using multiple progressive enviro-fascist sources in an incredibly detailed video[210].

Are plastic bags even 'single-use', though?

They Fear Unity

The legislation that leftists typically propose in their mission to ban plastic bags, straws, and other items generally refers to plastic[211] as 'single-use'. This implies that the plastic is not used again or recycled by the consumer. One New Hampshire bill[212] was titled *'to eliminate single-use plastic carry-out bags'*. But in reality, we all know that after using them to carry groceries home from the store, nearly every American reuses their plastic bags at least once more. They are often used as garbage bags for small trash cans throughout the home, to carry items when going out or traveling, to pick up after the dog while on walks, and for many other purposes. I regularly use these 'single-use' plastic bags for a variety of jobs around the house and at work. Additionally, a large and increasing percentage of the plastic used throughout the world is being recycled, according to the data provided earlier. I'm sure that many of these bags are actually made from recycled plastic, and may even be reincarnated to live multiple lives! Recycled and reusable products represent the exact antithesis of 'single-use', do they not? So, should anti-freedom zealots stop calling them by this inaccurate pejorative?

Progressive lawmakers also propose bills that would ban styrofoam[213]. The Green Dining Alliance[214] recently published an article titled *'Polystyrene Fact Sheet: 8 reasons to ban Styrofoam'*. By 2019, politicians in over 100 cities[215] and counties throughout the union banned styrofoam, according to Freedonia Focus Reports.

Once progressives successfully criminalize the use of plastic, paper, cardboard, and styrofoam, take-out and many other conveniences will essentially become illegal. This will anger many consumers. Enviro-fascists have hated those who use the 'dirty' materials for years, but once they are criminalized, those who relied on them for daily living will also begin to hate the enviro-fascists who banned the useful materials. This will create more division between neighbors, which plays right into the hands of the politicians and the elites.

Modern environmentalists are also waging an all-out war against fossil fuels[216]. They want oil, gasoline, and coal to be banned. They want everyone to be forced to use 'renewable' energy to power everything, including their vehicles and their homes. California will require all vehicles to be electric by 2035[217] and other progressive states are expected to pass similar laws. Of course, the mining process for the electric car batteries is horrifically inhumane[218] and very unenvironmental[219], not to mention that they are prohibitively expensive[220] to replace. Additionally, the charging stations that keep the 'green' vehicles running (remember, you'll need to charge them for around 30 minutes[221] in order to drive 50-100 miles) are literally powered by fossil fuels[222]! Renewable (non-scarce) energy such as solar, wind, and hydroelectric are not capable of powering the vehicles, and can't come close to powering the entire grid. So, the 'green' cars charge at power stations that use energy created by fossil fuels.

The progressives have also been promoting windmills as a panacea to reversing global warming. Again, the scientific facts demonstrate that they are a net negative for the environment, even if only analyzed from a 'fossil-fuel-use' or 'energy-efficiency' perspective. Building windmills requires a tremendous amount of materials and energy. Think about the energy required to manufacture, transport, and assemble thousands of tons of metal. Think about all of the other materials and wiring that go into the structures. Never mind that massive concrete foundations must first be laid beneath the windmill in order to keep them erect. If you believe that pouring tons of concrete has no environmental impact, you just might be naive enough to vote for global warming alarmists. An excellent essay[223] outlined how energy-intensive it is to construct the enormous windmills. A few of the figures include:

- *Excavate a 10-feet deep, 100-feet wide hole. Excavators use 14 liters of diesel per hour. No big deal!*
- *Set 96,000 pounds of reinforcing steel rebar for the windmill base into the concrete.*
- *53 concrete trucks pour foundations. If each truck can haul 8 cubic yards at 2,538 lbs/yard * 53 = 1,076,112 pounds = 538 tons.*
- *Move cranes to the site and operate them for hundreds of hours, and then build, transport, and construct the actual structure, which stands at a few hundred feet in height.*
- *If the windmill is in the sea, ships are required to transport the parts, and setting an underwater foundation for the windmills is even more complicated, expensive, dangerous, unenvironmental, and energy-consuming.*

Watching a video on windmill construction[224] is likely to convince any enviro-fascist that they could not possibly be energy-efficient endeavors. They are certainly impressive feats of science and architecture, but constructing one is not very different from building a skyscraper from an energy-consumption perspective.

Maintaining the windmills (including using helicopters to clean and de-ice the turbine blades) also requires a lot of energy, time, and money. And windmills have a lifetime of only 15-20 years. And Disposing of the massive hunks of metal is so problematic that even progressive publications[225] have admitted that their size, weight, and strength make them unfathomably challenging to disassemble and recycle or bury. They don't produce enough energy to offset their energy cost, and they likely would not be a net producer of energy even if the wind did blow constantly - which it does not. Once again, the activists who claim to love nature and animals are responsible for killing large numbers of bats and birds[226] and disrupting marine wildlife[227] in numerous ways. The large turbines also take up a lot of space that could otherwise be put to productive use, and they make so much noise that the Union of

Concerned Scientists admitted in a paper[228] that *"some people living close to wind facilities have complained about sound and vibration issues."*

A helicopter de-ices windmill turbines in one of the most ironic photographs on the internet

Progressives claim to believe the seas are rapidly rising due to man-made global warming caused by the mythical 'greenhouse gas phenomenon', yet they continue moving to and investing in beach cities. And anyone who points out any issues with their preferred energy production methods or acknowledges their hypocritical behavior is treated like the enemy. More division.

Despite their ideology being rooted in hypocrisy[229], nihilism, and science denial, these radical environmentalists' hatred for the opposition continues to grow. And who is their opposition? It's anyone who does not believe that humans are causing catastrophic global warming that necessitates strict laws controlling our 'carbon footprint'. It's anyone who believes that the Earth exists to benefit humanity, and not vice versa. If you believe in the ideas of Genesis - that God created the Earth so that it could serve humanity - you are definitely their enemy. I am personally agnostic, but I believe that humans are superior to the Earth. Of course, I believe that we should be the best stewards of the Earth as we can be, but that does not mean that we must place its health over ours or that we should sacrifice our health and prosperity to benefit the environment. I love clean air, and I wish nothing was in the ocean except for natural sea life. But I do not support abolishing all viable energy sources and all humans to realize those goals. What's disturbing is that radical leftists and elites seem to believe that humans should be culled for the benefit of the planet. Over the past few years, they have made this very clear. Increasingly, we have seen radical environmentalists lash out at normal people -

humans who believe in humanity. Joe Biden and congressional Democrats constantly attack fossil fuel producers and threaten to eliminate them[230]. A major part of the progressives' Green New Deal is painting those who use fossil fuels as evil[231] people who want to bring about the destruction of the world[232].

Many prominent leftists have made it a point to publicly announce that they will not be reproducing[233]. Why bring more Earth-killing producers of carbon dioxide into this world when it is such a toxic substance to the planet's agriculture? (Never mind that carbon dioxide is literally plant-fuel just like oxygen is human-fuel.) Even back in 2017, NBC[234] was publishing articles like *'Science proves kids are bad for Earth. Morality suggests we stop having them.'*

These sociopaths believe that humans are inherently evil and destructive. Humans who have children[235] are not spared from the scorn of radical environmentalists. Indeed, many progressives believe that humans are a virus[236] that is killing the planet. Some Democrat lawmakers have already proposed legislation that would limit each couple to three children[237]. In 2023, a prominent medical journal[238] published an article advocating for medicine to focus less on humans and more on 'ecological equity'. The authors believe that *"all life is equal, and of equal concern...requires a complete change to our relationship with animals...from an animal-based diet to a plant-based one, which not only benefits human health, but also animal health and wellbeing."* While asserting that humans are not more important than animals, the buffoons push for people to eat plants - which takes away food from the animals they claim to love. Furthermore, some plants are nearly as alive and sentient[239] as some animals. Does that mean that humans should stop eating plants, too? Should we live off of unicorn excrement and rainbows?

It's only a matter of time before these radical extremists begin using violence to attack the people they see as the greatest current threat to their world. We have all surely seen the increasingly common clashes[240] between enviro-fascists and the people who they consider 'climate criminals'. Some environmental activists seem to be open to using violence[241] in their mission to eliminate fossil fuels and anything else that they consider damaging to their environment. Disturbingly, nearly every major government in the world now claims that global warming is man-made and is the greatest menace to mankind. And many elites are considering more corona-fascism-style lockdowns[242] for the 'environmental emergency' that is global warming. During lockdowns, carbon production plummets. And when the environment is your top priority, no measure is too extreme!

The attacks against pro-humanity people are growing more vicious by the day. It's only a matter of time before retaliation begins to occur. Once the lockdowns begin, a counter-attack may be imminent. Once normal vehicles are banned and electric vehicles are mandated, this civil war may escalate.

This divider is working very well for the elites, who are sitting back in their private jets and beach homes laughing at the peasants who are busy fighting each other and ignoring the greatest tyrants - and polluters - in the world. Interestingly, DC politicians and the federal government are terribly damaging to both humanity and the environment. They increasingly violate human rights and harm the environment at a preposterous scale. Studies have found that the DC empire is the biggest polluter in the world, largely due to its tremendous military, which includes the regular testing of bombs, which are terrible for the environment[243]. Of course, DC's endless military violence in every part of the world is responsible for killing many humans[244], as well.

> **Axios** @axios
>
> Climate change is among Latinos' leading concerns heading into the midterm elections, according to an Axios-Ipsos Latino poll in partnership with Noticias Telemundo.
>
> axios.com
> Climate change among top concerns for Latinos ahead of midterms, poll finds
> Latinos in the U.S. are especially affected by the consequences of climate change, research finds.
>
> 7:57 AM · Nov 5, 2022 · SocialFlow
>
> 12 Retweets   76 Quote Tweets   63 Likes
>
> **Carnovich** @Carnovich · 5h
> Replying to @axios
> lol no it's not
> 49   87   1,953

Chapter 11: The Exception To The Rule

We have demonstrated that the Marxist strategy utilized by the elites attacks family units, gatherings, and communities. Simply put, those in power fear unity, so they keep us divided. However, those in charge do promote some forms of unity and certain types of gatherings.

While gathering at churches and other places of worship is constantly attacked by the progressive left and was even prohibited under corona-fascism, gathering for the purpose of protesting against freedom (or in support of tyranny) is applauded by politicians, for obvious reasons.

At the height of the scamdemic, when anti-freedom BLM activists engaged in 'mostly violent' protests, politicians ignored corona-fascism and supported the protests[245]. Some politicians went as far as joining[246] the actual protests. All Democrats and even some Republicans[247] endorsed BLM and their Marxist agenda. The purported agenda of BLM is to call for police accountability, but Democrat and Republican leaders don't actually support that. And BLM leaders are seemingly content with the politicians' lip service regarding accountability for bad cops. But BLM's real agenda is to diminish freedom, empower the government (which includes the police), fuel the animosity toward white people, and shift the government ever closer to Marxism. And this part of their agenda is supported by nearly every politician and 99% of Congress (only Rand Paul and Thomas Massie generally seem to oppose authoritarian Marxism).

Under corona-fascism, gathering in a house or restaurant with your biological family is a crime and must be condemned and prohibited, but politicians and leftists can gather with other leftists as much as they desire. The socialists can unite, but those who love liberty must be kept apart from one another.

To make the rules clear:

Conservatives, libertarians, voluntaryists, and pro-freedom individuals must be condemned for gathering or forming any sort of community. Church communities are bigoted. Gun clubs are fascist. Home school communities are considered child abuse. Parents are not necessary - the politicians and other government officials are the trusted adults who will raise and educate[248] your children. Some government school employees may even execute the CDC's learning objectives[249] and convince your child that they are transgendered!

Anti-freedom leftists are encouraged to unite and gather and form socialist, feminist, and anti-conservative communities. In fact, such institutions should be endorsed by Americans and should receive taxpayer dollars, according to leftists.

But is everyone in the union okay with these new societal rules?

Are all 340,000,000 people in all 50 states okay with endorsing leftist communities while condemning conservative, religious, and libertarian communities?

Why is it okay to gather and worship the government, but unacceptable to gather with family or attend religious or pro-liberty events?

We are living in a society comprised of at least two different groups of people. In fact, there may be three or maybe even dozens of fundamentally distinct groups within the united states.

A nation can only survive if all its residents have a congruous value system. In the 50 states that comprise this union, however, we have one group that is authoritarian, socialist, and opposed to nearly all forms of freedom, including gun rights, school choice, economic freedom, free speech, and more. Another group supports those same freedoms and prioritizes those freedoms above everything else, including equality, safety, and unity. Could one nation really survive when its people are split into multiple groups with such conflicting worldviews?

Chapter 12: How United Are We?

The elites seek to divide their constituents based on their many characteristics. Yet, people often get along very well with those who look and act differently. But the truth is that when it comes to the most important policy issues, the 340 million inhabitants of the united states do not agree. Depending on the particular issue, the people throughout the union are split in two, three, or more ways. Additionally, DC politicians have proven for decades to be terribly out of touch with many or most of the people living normal lives.

From 2016-2022, over 250,000 respondents[250] to the question 'Do you think abortion should be legal or illegal?' provided the following results:

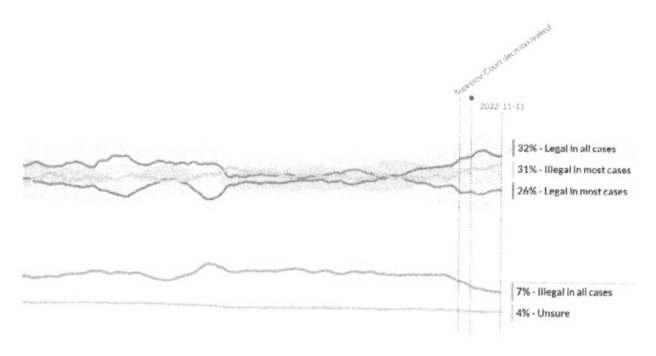

2022-11-11 Supreme Court decision leaked

32% - Legal in all cases
31% - Illegal in most cases
26% - Legal in most cases
7% - Illegal in all cases
4% - Unsure

As of this writing, 58% believe that abortion should be permitted in all or most cases, while 38% believe that it should be prohibited in all or most cases. Does that sound like a union in which everyone is satisfied and united in their beliefs?

From 2017-2022, 227,000 respondents[251] to the question 'Do you have a favorable or unfavorable opinion of Joe Biden?' provided the following results:

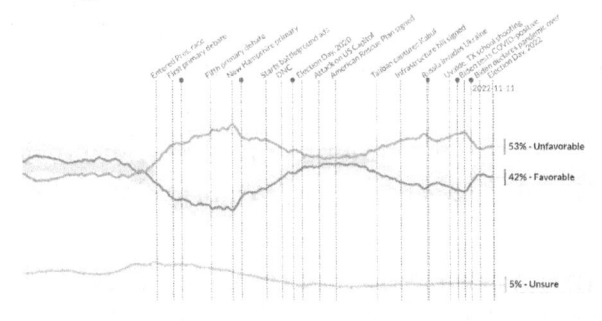

As of this writing, 53% of Americans disapprove of the President, and 42% approve of him. Does that sound like a union in which everyone is satisfied and united in their beliefs?

From 2015-2022, 788,000 respondents[252] to the question 'How would you rate the condition of the national economy right now?' provided the following results:

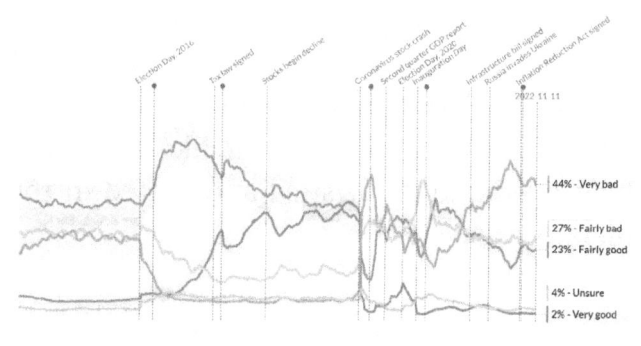

As of this writing, 71% of Americans believe that the economy is bad, and 25% believe that it is good. That means that two facts must be true: The majority of people do not approve of the government-controlled economy of the united states, which is controlled almost entirely by the federal government, and that there is not a clear consensus among all Americans.

From 2017-2022, 452,000 respondents[253] to the question 'Do you think things in this country are headed in the right direction, or have they gotten off on the wrong track?' provided the following results:

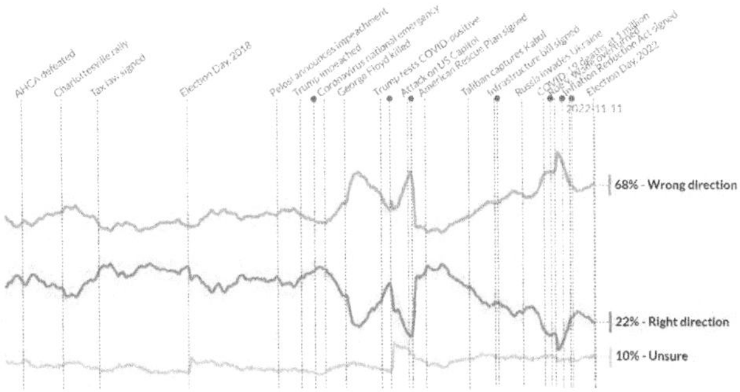

As of this writing, 68% of Americans believe that the union of states is on the wrong track, while 22% believe that the union is headed in the right direction. Again, this makes two facts extremely clear: Americans do not believe that the union can remain intact, and they hate the way DC politicians rule over all 340,000,000 unique individuals in the united states.

Over the past two years, 397,000 respondents[254] to the question 'How concerned are you about a coronavirus outbreak in your local area?' provided the following results:

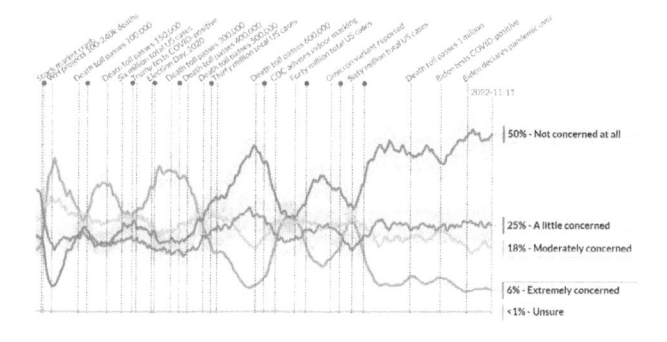

As of this writing, 50% of Americans are not at all concerned about COVID. In April 2020, only 8% were not at all concerned about the virus, indicating that people are becoming less worried about its danger as time goes on. Yet, (again, at the time of this writing) DC politicians are now implementing more authoritarian corona-fascist rules than ever before. Additionally, this survey also shows an important fact: There is no clear consensus among the people of the united states; they are horribly split on this issue, as they are on nearly all major issues. The survey currently shows that 25% of people are 'a little concerned', 18% of people are 'moderately concerned', and 6% of people are 'extremely concerned'. Remember, 50% are 'not concerned at all'. How could all of those people live under one set of laws?

They Fear Unity

From 2017-2022, 359,000 respondents[255] to the question 'Do you support or oppose the Black Lives Matter movement?' provided the following results:

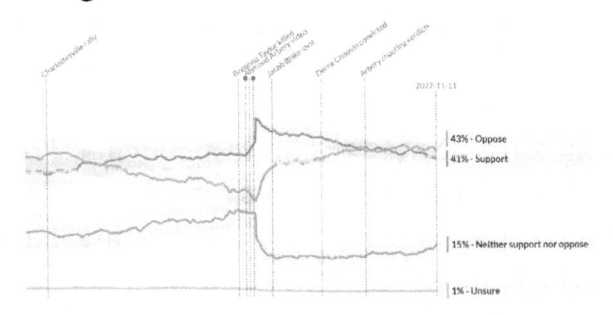

43% - Oppose
41% - Support
15% - Neither support nor oppose
1% - Unsure

As of this writing, 41% of Americans support BLM and 43% oppose the Marxist anti-white movement. This makes one thing very clear: we are not all united. We are as divided as we could possibly be. Is the solution forcing us all to live together or letting states go their separate ways?

From 2015-2022, 293,000 respondents[256] to the question 'Do you favor or oppose stricter gun control laws?' provided the following results:

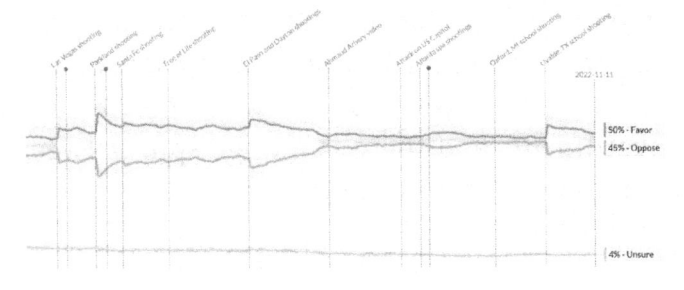

50% - Favor
45% - Oppose
4% - Unsure

As of this writing, 50% of people in the united states want to pass stricter gun control laws, while 45% do not want stricter gun control laws. If that does not indicate that the people throughout the united states are divided on the issue of guns, I can't imagine what would.

From 2015-2022, 433,000 respondents[257] to the question 'Do you have a favorable or unfavorable opinion of the Democratic Party?' provided the following results:

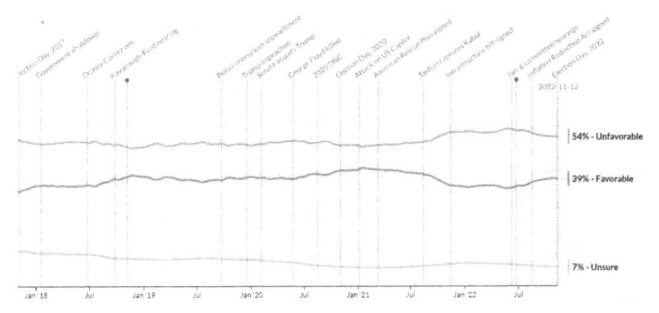

As of this writing, only 39% of respondents said they have a favorable opinion of the Democratic Party – the party that as of this writing controls all parts of Washington DC, while 54% have an unfavorable opinion of the Democrats. Again, this makes two things very clear: most people in the united states do not like the federal government, and there is a huge split between the two sides of the united states.

From 2017-2022, 234,000 respondents[258] to the question 'Do you think that the use of cannabis should be legal, or not?' provided the following results:

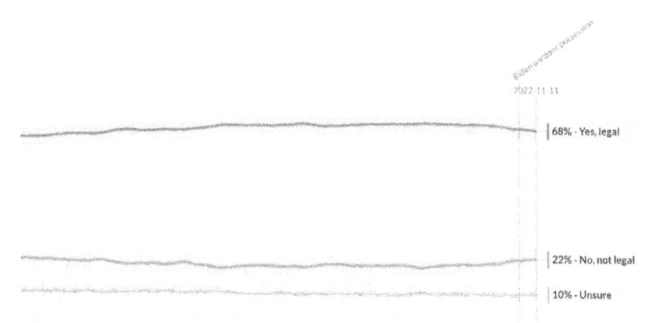

```
———————————————————————————— | 68% - Yes, legal

———————————————————————————— | 22% - No, not legal
                                | 10% - Unsure
```

As of this writing, 68% said they believe that it should be legal, while 22% said that it should remain illegal. Currently, the benevolent geniuses in DC still have cannabis listed as a 'schedule 1' prohibited substance, which is the most severe designation possible for any substance. DC politicians still believe that cannabis is one of the most dangerous substances in existence, despite the majority of Americans believing the exact opposite. Yet, some people continue to believe that the federal government perfectly represents the will of all 340 million people, in all 50 states.

From 2016-2022, 283,000 respondents[259] to the question 'Should the United States deport immigrants living here illegally or offer them a path to citizenship?' provided the following results:

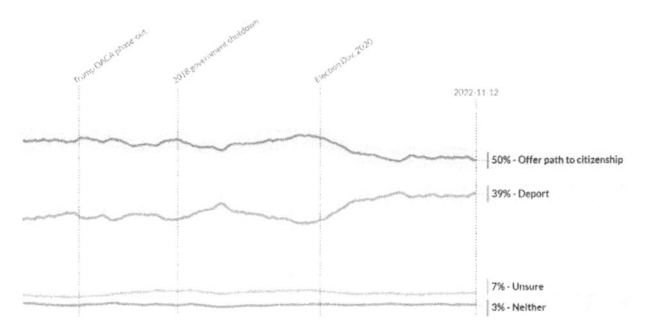

As of this writing, 39% said that the illegal aliens should be deported, while 50% said that they should be offered a path to citizenship. Does that sound like a united opinion or a divided opinion? How could one federal government make one legal determination that adequately satisfies both sides of this critical issue? Regardless of what the government decides, one side will feel terribly betrayed by their government.

From 2018-2022, 188,000 respondents[260] to the question 'Do you support or oppose raising taxes on the wealthy?' provided the following results:

They Fear Unity

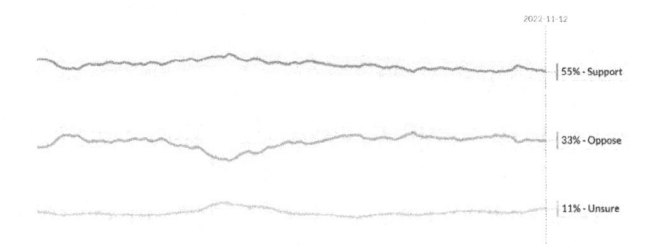

```
2023-11-12
───────────────────────── 55% - Support
───────────────────────── 33% - Oppose
───────────────────────── 11% - Unsure
```

As of this writing, 55% said that they do support raising taxes, while 33% oppose increasing taxes. One thing is clear: We do not all agree on whether taxation should exist and how high it should be.

The same divisive findings apply to opinions about governmental control of the environment[261], universal healthcare[262], universal basic income[263], a government-guaranteed job[264], and much more.

Chapter 13: Unity Through Division

Power-hungry politicians and their elite cronies have made it clear that they intend to use division to keep us under their thumb for the foreseeable future. While not all of their strategies to divide us have worked as well as they hoped, they have managed to sow a high level of division between many cohorts throughout the 50 states. As long as they continue to divide large groups of people and turn them against their neighbors, we will never unite as one singular country. Even if unity were possible, it's hard to imagine ever being able to fix the federal government. So, what should we do to combat their 'divide and control' tactics? It's impossible to coexist with one another, and few people have the desire to coexist with those they consider to have destructive or disturbing values.

Along with my colleagues and mentors, I have been warning for years that the united states are all on the American bus, which is rapidly headed toward annihilation. Not only are we all headed for certain doom, but we are killing each other and making one another miserable during the ride. Some see us as being on a bus that is being driven toward a steep cliff. When

Democrats are in charge, the bus tends to travel very rapidly. When Republicans are elected and gain control of the bus, they do not turn it around. They do not even stop the bus from driving us all to hell. At best, they slow down the bus and keep us on the path to doom at a slightly slower speed than the opposition party. Progressive voters would likely say that the Republicans drive the bus to hell faster than the Democrats.

For more than 100 years, Republican politicians have proven that they endorse tyranny and oppose liberty nearly as much as their Democrat colleagues. No Republican will be our Lord and Savior. I said this before Trump, it was proven throughout his presidency, and I believe it to be true today more than ever. Republicans will not save us and they certainly cannot unite or 'fix' the union or DC. Tyranny will only ever continue to proliferate, emanating from DC like a malignant tumor. And this tyranny is largely enabled by the 'divide and control' strategy that the elites love to utilize. We are clearly headed for destruction. Remember, only around 15% of people in the united states believe that we are heading in the right direction.

What do we do when our vehicle totally loses traction and begins to carry us toward certain death?

We steer into the skid.

Let's use their momentum against them. The elites stoke division. Let's concede. Let's use their blueprint. We don't need to agree with their manufactured race-war or gender-war, but we can use their divisiveness against them. Progressives, conservatives, and libertarians truly are too different to share one society that has one set of rules. Let's make this fact known to the elites. Gun owners cannot live with gun-grabbers. Religious people who believe in the sanctity of life cannot live in the same country as those who enjoy, praise, and applaud the killing of babies, even when they are mere seconds from birth (or even during or after birth). People like me who believe that taxation is immoral, impractical, and unnecessary theft[265] cannot coexist with those who believe they're entitled to take my money and control my property.

We must find a way to use their own arguments - about how evil libertarians and conservatives are - to defeat them. Once we convince enough people in the united states that there are indeed many diverse groups and that it is perfectly reasonable to prefer to live among like-minded people, we can defeat tyranny.

Once we successfully split the union into two, three, 20, or 50 independent states, we will have won. Once we are living in sovereign states, we will no longer be ruled by DC; we would be governed only by those in our own state, who are much more likely to share our values and much more beholden to our opinions. If a person finds himself stuck in a state that does not share his values (a libertarian in New York, for instance), he could simply move to another state and escape that tyranny. Currently, moving from New York to New Hampshire only solves the problem of New York's tyrannical and abusive laws, but it does nothing to protect people from DC politicians and federal law enforcement. Once each state disassociates from the sociopaths in DC, moving to New Hampshire - which is already the freest state[266] - would improve a person's liberty and quality of life immediately and drastically.

Conversely, all the socialists living in conservative states would be free to move to

New Jersey, which could continue their socialist anti-freedom policies even as a sovereign nation. In fact, an independent New Jersey could finally legalize cannabis and improve police accountability, universal healthcare, socialism, social justice, and due process[267] once DC no longer has any influence over its policies. Breaking up the union would have tremendous benefits for all 50 states.

My favorite reasons for cutting ties with DC?

I would no longer be forced by the threat of violence to fund my own abuse and the abuse of my neighbors by some of the most divisive and controlling tyrants to ever walk this planet: DC politicians. I would no longer be forced by armed agents of the state to fund infinite wars, surveillance, and crimes all over the world. I would no longer be forced to send billions of dollars to corrupt politicians in Ukraine, Iran, South Korea, and the other 180 countries of the world. I would finally be able to possess suppressors and short-barrelled rifles. I would no longer be forced to fund dystopian gain-of-function research that could lead to pandemics and corona-fascism[268]. I would no longer be forced to pay for checkpoints like the ones conducted by CBP, ICE, and local police whenever DC politicians send them millions of dollars to conduct 'sobriety checkpoints'. I would enjoy escaping from the tyranny of the DC empire for over 100 more reasons[269].

But that's just me.

You may not feel the same way. And that is perfectly okay. You may actually think that I'm a dangerous lunatic...which proves my point: we really should not live together under one roof if we each think the other is crazy and a threat to our lives.

The End

Thank you so much for reading my book about unity and division! I must thank my wife for her incredible and unwavering support and my father for being the #1 proofreader I know. I really hope that you found some value in it. If you did, please share it with a friend and please leave a review when you get a chance. It helps others find the book and learn the important lessons it teaches. If you would like to follow my latest projects, please visit LibertyBlock.com and listen to The Liberty Block podcast.

- Alu

They Fear Unity

Recommended reading

Presumed Guilty – Elliot "Alu" Axelman
Taxation Is Theft – Elliot "Alu" Axelman
The Plague That Must Not Be Questioned – Elliot "Alu" Axelman
The Progressive Solution – Elliot "Alu" Axelman & Marcus Ruiz Evans
Articles of Secession – Elliot "Alu" Axelman
The Blueprint For Liberty – Elliot "Alu" Axelman
Secret Empires – Peter Schweizer
1984 – George Orwell
The Myth of the Rational Voter – Bryan Caplan
Dumbing Us Down – John Taylor Gatto
The Fountainhead – Ayn Rand
Government – The Biggest Scam In History – Howard Lichtman
Follow The Money – Dan Bongino
Pandemia – Alex Berenson
Shadow Bosses – Mallory Factor
The Creature From Jekyll Island – G. Edward Griffin
End The Fed – Ron Paul
The Case Against Education – Bryan Caplan
Animal Farm – George Orwell
The Moral Case For Fossil Fuels – Alex Epstein
Human Action – Ludwig Von Mises
Atlas Shrugged – Ayn Rand
Fahrenheit 451 – Ray Bradbury
Man, Economy, & State – Murray Rothbard
Texit – Daniel Miller
Basic Economics – Thomas Sowell
Wealth of Nations – Adam Smith
The Law – Frédéric Bastiat
Economics In One Lesson – Henry Hazlitt
Rich Dad Poor Dad – Robert Kiyosaki
Faucian Bargain – Steve Deace & Todd Erzen
Common Sense: The Case For An Independent Texas – Bob Murphy
Blue Dawn – Blaine Pardoe
The Next Civil War – Stephen Marche
The Definitive Guide to Libertarian Voluntaryism – Jack Lloyd
Tony's Virus – Steven Greer
The Real Anthony Fauci – Robert F. Kennedy
A Plague Upon Our House – Scott Atlas
The Ecstatic Pessimist – Carla Gericke

Alu Axelman

Any tip would be greatly appreciated!

PayPal	Venmo
paypal.me/EAxelman	
Bitcoin Cash (BCH)	Bitcoin (BTC)
DASH	Monero (XMR)

Endnotes

1. https://libertyblock.com/the-non-representative-republic
2. https://townhall.com/tipsheet/mattvespa/2020/07/07/usa-today-twists-itself-into-a-pretzel-trying-to-deny-democratic-party-roots-in-civil-war-and-the-kkk-n2571980
3. https://www.history.com/topics/reconstruction/ku-klux-klan
4. https://www.hellomisterbrown.com/blog/the-content-of-their-character-mlk-quote
5. https://redstate.com/mike_miller/2020/10/24/washington-state-library-fights-racism-with-segregated-race-sensitivity-training-n268407
6. https://www.foxnews.com/us/seattle-chop-segregated-training-session-white-supremacy-physical-safety
7. https://www.theblaze.com/news/columbia-6-segregated-graduation-ceremonies
8. https://www.eeoc.gov/eeoc/history/35th/thelaw/eo-10925.html
9. https://www.law.cornell.edu/wex/affirmative_action
10. https://www.eeoc.gov/laws/statutes/titlevii.cfm
11. https://youtu.be/X4b77yvDzlw
12. https://www.law.cornell.edu/supremecourt/text/438/265
13. youtube.com/watch?v=cEzSvagZ_60
14. whitedate.net/how-many-white-people-are-there-in-the-world

15. theguardian.com/us-news/2021/aug/12/us-2020-census-white-population-declines
16. https://www.breitbart.com/politics/2021/04/22/senate-democrats-vote-to-allow-asian-racial-discrimination-in-higher-education
17. dailycaller.com/2023/01/19/17-northern-virginia-schools-withheld-merit-awards-asian-students-legislation
18. cnn.com/2023/01/16/us/fairfax-county-virginia-schools-investigation/index.html
19. ibtimes.com/white-black-crime-vs-black-white-crime-new-statistics-show-more-killings-between-2424598
20. https://youtu.be/u85kXAxYeQ8?t=39
21. theroot.com/whiteness-is-a-pandemic-1846494770
22. vox.com/2016/2/12/10978126/democratic-debate-racial-justice
23. pewresearch.org/fact-tank/2022/11/28/black-and-white-americans-are-far-apart-in-their-views-of-reparations-for-slavery
24. congress.gov/bill/116th-congress/house-bill/40/cosponsors?searchResultViewType=expanded
25. reuters.com/article/us-usa-biden-slavery/white-house-says-biden-supports-study-of-slavery-reparations-idUSKBN2AH2K9
26. sfreparations.org/documents
27. nypost.com/2023/01/16/sf-reparations-panel-proposes-5m-lump-sum-payment-to-eligible-residents
28. thedailybeast.com/kamala-harris-ag-office-tried-to-keep-inmates-locked-up-for-cheap-labor

29. prisonjournalismproject.org/2022/08/05/california-prisons-forced-labor-lives-on

30. mayoclinic.org/diseases-conditions/coronavirus/expert-answers/coronavirus-infection-by-race/faq-20488802

31. now.tufts.edu/articles/why-people-color-are-suffering-more-covid-19

32. bostonreview.net/science-nature-race/bram-wispelwey-michelle-morse-antiracist-agenda-medicine

33. americanthinker.com/articles/2021/04/medical_racism__preferential_treatments_for_blacks_over_whites___is_here.html

34. thelancet.com/journals/lancet/article/PIIS0140-6736(21)00775-3/fulltext

35. nejm.org/race-and-medicine

36. wbur.org/commonhealth/2020/10/28/united-against-racism-boston-hospital-plan

37. libertyblock.com/the-empires-medical-system-is-becoming-disturbingly-racist

38. https://khn.org/news/article/vermont-gives-blacks-and-other-minority-residents-vaccine-priority

39. https://reason.com/2020/12/18/vaccine-cdc-essential-workers-elderly-racial-covid-19/

40. foxnews.com/media/critical-race-theory-related-ideas-found-mandatory-programs-58-top-100-us-medical-schools-report

41. forbes.com/sites/niallmccarthy/2017/03/07/the-massive-wage-gap-between-u-s-citizens-and-immigrants-infographic/?sh=6bad233d3e65

42. nytimes.com/interactive/2022/07/11/opinion/immigrants-success-america.html
43. hbr.org/2021/08/research-why-immigrants-are-more-likely-to-become-entrepreneurs
44. nfap.com/wp-content/uploads/2019/01/2018-BILLION-DOLLAR-STARTUPS.NFAP-Policy-Brief.2018-1.pdf
45. 12ft.io/proxy?&q=https%3A%2F%2Fwww.dailywire.com%2Fnews%2Fwalsh-are-cops-hunting-down-black-men-statistics-say-no
46. msn.com/en-us/news/us/opinion-the-police-who-killed-tyre-nichols-were-black-but-they-might-still-have-been-driven-by-racism
47. msnbc.com/morning-joe/watch/rev-al-tyre-nichols-death-is-an-outrage-and-race-is-still-involved-161680965819
48. flaglerlive.com/26685/gc-fdr-and-taxes
49. taxpolicycenter.org/statistics/historical-highest-marginal-income-tax-rates
50. freedomwire.com/obama-hypocrisy-multi-million-dollar-mansion
51. nypost.com/2016/01/18/hillary-clintons-caymans-tax-dodge-hypocrisy
52. financialpost.com/news/how-al-gore-amassed-a-200-million-fortune-after-presidential-defeat
53. amazon.com/Burn-Loot-Murder-Matter-Radical/dp/1087933803
54. theothermccain.com/2021/04/12/blm-buy-large-mansion

55. heritage.org/taxes/report/the-laffer-curve-past-present-and-future
56. youtu.be/28_jE8Yk2hc
57. howmuch.net/articles/high-income-americans-pay-majority-of-federal-taxes
58. reuters.com/article/us-usa-election-inequality-poll/majority-of-americans-favor-wealth-tax-on-very-rich-reuters-ipsos-poll-idUSKBN1Z9141
59. cbsnews.com/news/sen-elizabeth-warren-introduces-ultra-millionaire-tax-act
60. libertyblock.com/evil-tyrants-try-to-trick-people-into-supporting-massive-new-taxes
61. finance.yahoo.com/news/income-inequality-greatest-democratic-states-120000384.html
62. economist.com/graphic-detail/2013/05/28/the-examined-life?Fsrc=scn%2Fgp%2Fwl%2Fdc%2Fbetterlifeindex
63. forbes.com/sites/timworstall/2013/06/01/astonishing-numbers-americas-poor-still-live-better-than-most-of-the-rest-of-humanity
64. intellectualtakeout.org/blog/us-has-fattest-poor-people-world-why
65. youtu.be/sSBNxpUe2ks
66. youtube.com/watch?v=UbueX92CKPk
67. youtube.com/watch?v=t2XFh_tD2RA
68. gaycenter.org/about/lgbtq
69. youtu.be/5KR_FOHir-Y
70. youtu.be/hfxwRUYeBfk
71. cnbc.com/2019/11/18/chick-fil-a-drops-donations-to-christian-charities-after-lgbt-protests.html

72. https://www.buzzfeed.com/pablovaldivia/x-things-that-100-straight-culture
73. thelibertarianrepublic.com/new-york-can-fine-you-250k-for-misgendering-somebody
74. adflegal.org/selina-soule-track-athlete-story
75. steroidabuse.com/testosterone-injection.html
76. newsweek.com/transgender-threat-womens-sports-opinion-1540418
77. boysvswomen.com
78. cbssports.com/soccer/news/a-dallas-fc-under-15-boys-squad-beat-the-u-s-womens-national-team-in-a-scrimmage
79. churchmilitant.com/news/article/man-dominates-female-powerlifting-record
80. nypost.com/2022/03/17/trans-swimmer-lia-thomas-wins-womens-500-yard-ncaa-title
81. espn.com/espn/feature/story/_/id/31681454/the-power-layshia-clarendon
82. youtu.be/4U4KGz72SEg
83. sportskeeda.com/mma/news-when-transgender-fighter-fallon-fox-broke-opponent-s-skull-mma-fight
84. nypost.com/2021/09/11/transgender-fighter-alana-mclaughlin-wins-mma-debut
85. savewomenssports.com
86. adflegal.org/FairPlay
87. iwv.org/campaign/protect-womens-sports
88. concernedwomen.org
89. savewomenssports.com/about/f/abbot-signs-law-protecting-female-athletes

90. savewomenssports.com/about/f/florida-gov-ron-desantis-signed-the-fairness-in-womens-sport-act
91. savewomenssports.com/about/f/idaho-governor-stands-up-for-females---signs-hb-500
92. savewomenssports.com/about/f/mississippi-passes-bill-to-protect-female-sports
93. savewomenssports.com/about/f/victory-for-girls-in-arkansas
94. savewomenssports.com/about/f/montana-governor-signs-bill-to-protect-female-athletes
95. thepostmillennial.com/arizona-laws-protect-kids-womens-sports-unborn-election-integrity
96. breitbart.com/sports/2022/03/03/iowa-gov-kim-reynolds-signs-bill-protecting-girls-sports-from-transgender-athletes
97. wlky.com/article/kentucky-transgender-sports-bill-now-law/39716594
98. thepostmillennial.com/tn-passes-bill-protect-girls-womens-sports
99. concernedwomen.org/south-carolina-makes-it-sweet-16-states-with-laws-that-protect-female-athletes
100. oklahoma.gov/governor/newsroom/newsroom/2022/march2022/governor-stitt-signs--save-women-s-sports-act--into-law.html
101. pjmedia.com/news-and-politics/athena-thorne/2022/03/27/utah-legislature-overrides-gov-cox-veto-passes-law-to-protect-girls-athletics-n1584707
102. thegatewaypundit.com/2021/04/alabama-governor-signs

-law-protecting-female-k-12-athletes-bans-biological-males-competing
103. gopusa.com/west-virginia-governor-signs-law-to-protect-girls-sports
104. breitbart.com/politics/2021/03/09/south-dakota-gov-kristi-noem-sign-bill-keeping-girls-sports-biological-females
105. americanprinciplesproject.org/legislation/veto-override-makes-indiana-17th-state-protect-girls-sports
106. iga.in.gov/legislative/2022/bills/house/1041
107. dailywire.com/news/using-the-term-birthing-people-erases-women
108. nypost.com/2021/05/11/sorry-but-theyre-called-mothers-not-birthing-people
109. equalinlife.com/blog/people-who-menstruate
110. eviemagazine.com/post/biological-male-wins-miss-greater-derry-beauty-pageant-america-transgender
111. kiiky.com/miss-america-scholarship
112. eviemagazine.com/post/women-disagree-pro-trans-movement-threats-violence-death
113. thehill.com/homenews/state-watch/559293-mayor-truck-running-into-pride-parade-was-a-terrorist-attack-against-the?rl=1
114. lifesitenews.com/blogs/he-was-a-transgender-toddler-at-3-rebaptized-as-girl-at-7
115. news.com.au/lifestyle/parenting/kids/texas-jury-rules-against-dad-trying-to-stop-sevenyearold-sons-gender-transition/news-story/72de8b437a6c4af0e60ffdd12a5c0ce4

They Fear Unity

116. theblaze.com/news/california-teachers-accused-of-secretly-coaching-gender-transition
117. thenationaldesk.com/news/americas-news-now/mom-scolds-california-school-for-allegedly-coaching-her-12-year-old-into-becoming-trans-spreckles-jessica-konen-transgender-lgbt-equality-clubs-teacher-student-gsa-gay-straight-alliance
118. dailydot.com/irl/straight-pride-day-twitter-hashtag-trolls
119. theguardian.com/society/2014/may/25/transgender-children-gender-identity-bigots-media
120. blog.peoplecount.org/evil-of-political-parties
121. responsiblestatecraft.org/2020/12/21/george-washington-warned-of-permanent-alliances-for-a-good-reason
122. washingtontimes.com/news/2022/dec/27/editorial-omnibus-bill-affirms-congress-budgeting-
123. atr.org/nearly-4000-epa-regulations-issued-under-president-obama
124. libertyblock.com/did-a-republican-senator-kill-a-pro-gun-bill
125. wikipedia.org/wiki/List_of_political_parties_in_the_United_States
126. independentpoliticalreport.com/2022/08/opinion-new-hampshire-ballot-access-needs-an-update
127. politico.com/magazine/story/2016/08/gary-johnson-debates-214168
128. libertyblock.com/americans-dont-want-a-queen-or-a-king
129. amzn.to/3K2452d

130. mynorthwest.com/2868545/rantz-inslee-brings-vaccine-passports-segregation-to-stadiums-colleges-churches
131. fox5ny.com/news/new-york-city-launches-vaccine-passport
132. libertyblock.com/masks-dont-work
133. libertyblock.com/disturbing-government-and-private-bribery-for-vaccination
134. libertyblock.com/legislation-makes-it-a-crime-to-disobey-citizen-mask-nazis
135. disrn.com/news/wisconsin-dnr-tells-employees-to-wear-masks-during-zoom-calls-at-home
136. joemduncan.medium.com/why-i-dont-feel-bad-when-anti-maskers-die-71d871f4bdda
137. trendingpolitics.com/i-want-to-beat-them-to-death-left-wing-journalist-threatens-anti-maskers-christians-during-unhinged-rant
138. wikipedia.org/wiki/List_of_people_burned_as_heretics
139. unamsanctamcatholicam.com/history/historical-apologetics/79-history/596-scientists-executed-by-the-catholic-church.html
140. nbcnews.com/news/us-news/california-pastor-church-found-contempt-fined-over-covid-rules-n1250481
141. bizpacreview.com/2020/10/12/orthodox-jewish-synagogues-in-nyc-fined-15000-for-having-more-than-10-people-inside-983560
142. nypost.com/2020/04/19/three-arrested-outside-nyc-synagogue-after-violating-social-distancing

143. buzzfeednews.com/article/dominicholden/coronavirus-drive-in-church-mississippi-lawsuit-trump
144. news.yahoo.com/full-video-gov-chris-sununu-151617031.html
145. nh.legal/Blog/lawsuit-filed-to-block-sununu-s-order-prohibiting-gatherings.html
146. courier-journal.com/story/news/2020/05/08/kentucky-coronavirus-judge-rules-churches-can-hold-person-services/3100142001/?fbclid=IwAR1y8KSvkrgO58yJEuLx0IJd05-zxfyGghsAo8pArQdUdPlIRUk_aq1Z6-E
147. usatoday.com/story/news/factcheck/2020/04/13/coronavirus-fact-check-ky-police-recorded-info-easter-churchgoers/2980574001
148. lifenews.com/2020/04/10/church-members-fined-500-each-for-attending-drive-in-service-but-abortion-clinics-can-still-kill-babies
149. libertyblock.com/scotus-takes-meaningless-2a-case
150. libertyblock.com/atf-all-guns-are-machine-guns
151. libertyblock.com/the-case-for-repealing-the-first-amendment
152. thetimesnews.com/opinion/20200313/williams-imposing-right-can-be-akin-to-theft
153. youtube.com/watch?v=koPmuEyP3a0
154. ncbi.nlm.nih.gov/pubmed/8477683
155. frontpagemag.com/feminism-killed-feminism
156. youtube.com/watch?v=LrhHkQhglig
157. thesun.co.uk/news/2690395/unhinged-feminist-youtuber-issues-crazed-call-for-women-to-kill-all-male-babies-and-any-man-you-see-in-the-streets
158. youtube.com/watch?v=-4S0gHlKiho

159. wikipedia.org/wiki/Education_Amendments_of_1972
160. deanclancy.com/a-list-of-colleges-that-dont-take-federal-money
161. innocenceproject.org/the-duke-lacrosse-case-and-a-career-goal
162. chronicle.com/article/my-title-ix-inquisition
163. nationalreview.com/2016/12/prof-claims-he-was-punished-sexual-misconduct-singing-beach-boys-song
164. thenation.com/article/archive/this-professor-was-fired-for-saying-fuck-no-in-class
165. media.ca7.uscourts.gov/cgi-bin/rssExec.pl?Submit=Display&Path=Y2014/D02-24/C:13-1757:J:Rovner:aut:T:fnOp:N:1295687:S:0
166. supreme.justia.com/cases/federal/us/503/60
167. ibtimes.com/white-black-crime-vs-black-white-crime-new-statistics-show-more-killings-between-2424598
168. dailywire.com/news/exit-poll-shows-nearly-70-of-single-women-voted-democrat-in-midterms
169. lifeisbeautiful.org/statistics-on-fatherless-homes
170. fatherhood.org/father-absence-statistic
171. heritage.org/welfare/report/how-welfare-undermines-marriage-and-what-do-about-it
172. newsmax.com/Newsfront/lois-lerner-irs-retire/2013/09/23/id/527223
173. nationalreview.com/2019/04/chick-fil-a-protests-anti-christian-mccarthyite
174. libertyblock.com/nh-judge-prohibiting-assembly-does-not-violate-constitution

175. nypost.com/2019/11/02/millennials-extreme-hatred-for-baby-boomers-is-totally-unjustified

176. vox.com/2019/5/22/18617686/baby-boomers-millennials-capitalism-joseph-sternberg

177. libertyblock.com/6-reasons-we-must-end-the-war-on-terror

178. theguardian.com/us-news/2020/jun/22/gen-z-hate-millennials-handy-guide-generation-wars

179. usatoday.com/story/news/politics/elections/2019/11/04/election-2020-young-voters-key-democrats-path-beating-trump/2458445001

180. whitehouse.gov/briefing-room/statements-releases/2022/08/24/fact-sheet-president-biden-announces-student-loan-relief-for-borrowers-who-need-it-most

181. forbes.com/advisor/student-loans/average-salary-college-graduates

182. news.yahoo.com/federal-judge-strikes-down-biden-005938514.html

183. washingtontimes.com%2Fnews%2F2022%2Faug%2F30%2Fbiden-buys-the-vote-with-student-loan-forgiveness

184. youtu.be/FK61bhBtVt4

185. forbes.com/sites/larrybell/2012/06/26/rising-tides-of-terror-will-melting-glaciers-flood-al-gores-coastal-home

186. cornwallalliance.org/2018/08/the-astonishing-failures-of-al-gores-arctic-prophecies

187. nasa.gov/feature/goddard/nasa-study-mass-gains-of-antarctic-ice-sheet-greater-than-losses

188. newsbusters.org/blogs/nb/noel-sheppard/2007/09/10/will-media-report-al-gores-hypocritical-private-plane-flights
189. worldpropertyjournal.com/featured-columnists/celebrity-homes-column-al-gore-tipper-gore-oprah-winfrey-michael-douglas-christopher-lloyd-fred-couples-nicolas-cage-peter-reckell-kelly-moneymaker-2525.php
190. celebritynetworth.com/richest-politicians/democrats/al-gore-net-worth
191. washingtonexaminer.com/opinion/on-this-date-51-years-ago-climate-scientists-predicted-a-new-ice-age-was-coming
192. foxnews.com/science/10-times-experts-predicted-the-world-would-end-by-now
193. greenpeace.org/usa/forests/solutions-to-deforestation
194. futureforestinc.com/six-benefits-of-logging-forests
195. dailysignal.com/2018/11/13/trump-is-right-poor-land-management-is-leading-to-bigger-california-fires
196. epa.gov/facts-and-figures-about-materials-waste-and-recycling/wood-material-specific-data
197. forest2market.com
198. ncsl.org/research/environment-and-natural-resources/plastic-bag-legislation
199. popsci.com/california-coffee-cancer-warning
200. 12ft.io/proxy?&q=https%3A%2F%2Fwww.theepochtimes.com%2Fsingle-use-plastic-tableware-to-be-banned-in-england_4954946.html
201. nj.com/news/2022/09/as-reusable-bags-pile-up-nj-considers-tweaking-plastic-bag-ban-to-allow-paper.html
202. wpst.com/paper-shopping-bags-new-jersey

203. bagtheban.com/in-your-state
204. fastcompany.com/40580132/here-are-the-u-s-cities-that-have-banned-plastic-straws-so-far
205. libertyblock.com/terrible-tuesday-at-the-state-house
206. legiscan.com/NH/text/HB558/id/1850158
207. legiscan.com/NH/votes/HB560/2019
208. ourworldindata.org/plastic-pollution
209. marinelitterthefacts.com/sources
210. youtu.be/O0tbn0F5X9U
211. libertyblock.com/should-plastic-be-banned
212. legiscan.com/NH/bill/HB1471/2022
213. libertyblock.com/nh-dems-want-to-ban-plastic-styrofoam
214. greendiningalliance.org/2015/10/8-reasons-to-ban-styro-foam
215. freedoniafocusreports.com/Content/Blog/2019/01/14/List-of-Cities-Banning-Polystyrene-Foam-Grows
216. theguardian.com/commentisfree/2021/mar/09/its-unavoidable-we-must-ban-fossil-fuels-to-save-our-planet-heres-how-we-do-it
217. bizpacreview.com/2022/09/05/states-consider-joining-california-in-mandating-all-electric-cars-by-2035-1281346
218. cbsnews.com/news/cobalt-children-mining-democratic-republic-congo-cbs-news-investigation
219. medium.com/a-balanced-transition/the-troubling-environmental-impacts-of-a-battery-related-mining-boom-c36a0c294e02
220. breitbart.com/tech/2022/10/20/the-green-tax-electric-vehicle-owners-shocked-by-battery-replacements-topping-20000

221. ucsusa.org/resources/electric-vehicle-charging-types-time-cost-and-savings
222. electricvehiclesfaqs.com/how-are-electric-car-charging-stations-powered
223. energyskeptic.com/2020/900-tons-of-material-to-build-just-1-windmill
224. youtu.be/IF40SuH7Qi0
225. npr.org/2019/09/10/759376113/unfurling-the-waste-problem-caused-by-wind-energy
226. National Wind Coordinating Committee (NWCC). 2010. Wind turbine interactions with birds, bats, and their habitats: A summary of research results and priority questions.
227. sharkresearch.earth.miami.edu/offshore-windmills-impact-on-the-marine-environment
228. ucsusa.org/resources/environmental-impacts-wind-power
229. libertyblock.com/even-leftists-know-that-global-warming-is-fake
230. atr.org/joe-biden-we-are-going-get-rid-fossil-fuels
231. dailywire.com/news/aoc-links-fossil-fuel-extraction-to-the-murder-rape-and-kidnapping-of-indigenous-women
232. therightscoop.com/aoc-oil-and-gas-are-fundamentally-incompatible-with-the-future-of-humanity
233. theatlantic.com/politics/archive/2021/09/millennials-babies-climate-change/620032
234. nbcnews.com/think/opinion/science-proves-kids-are-bad-earth-morality-suggests-we-stop-ncna820781

235. bigthink.com/surprising-science/humans-have-a-moral-duty-to-stop-procreating
236. theguardian.com/uk/2003/feb/14/environment.highereducation
237. fism.tv/house-democrat-introduces-legislation-requiring-forced-sterilization-three-child-limit
238. thelancet.com/journals/lancet/article/PIIS0140-6736(23)00090-9/fulltext
239. theguardian.com/environment/radical-conservation/2015/aug/04/plants-intelligent-sentient-book-brilliant-green-internet
240. reuters.com/business/energy/protesters-clash-with-police-enbridge-pipeline-construction-site-minnesota-2021-06-07
241. dw.com/en/disruptive-climate-protests-do-they-help-or-hinder/a-61379793
242. thehill.com/opinion/finance/592011-coming-soon-climate-lockdowns
243. theconversation.com/us-military-is-a-bigger-polluter-than-as-many-as-140-countries-shrinking-this-war-machine-is-a-must-119269
244. globalresearch.ca/us-has-killed-more-than-20-million-people-in-37-victim-nations-since-world-war-ii/5492051
245. dailymail.co.uk/news/article-8426963/PIERS-MORGAN-support-BLM-protests-no-right-say-Trumps-rally-canceled.html
246. fox4kc.com/news/lets-march-together-mayor-lucas-kneels-marches-with-kansas-city-protesters

247. cbsnews.com/news/mitt-romney-marches-black-lives-matter-protest-washington-dc
248. twitter.com/RepSwalwell/status/1590545381641060352
249. cdc.gov/healthyyouth/safe-supportive-environments/pd-lgbtq.htm
250. civiqs.com/results/abortion_legal?uncertainty=true&annotations=true&zoomIn=true
251. civiqs.com/results/favorable_joe_biden?uncertainty=true&annotations=true&zoomIn=true
252. civiqs.com/results/economy_us_now?uncertainty=true&annotations=true&zoomIn=true
253. civiqs.com/results/track_country?uncertainty=true&annotations=true&zoomIn=true
254. civiqs.com/results/coronavirus_concern?uncertainty=true&annotations=true&zoomIn=true
255. civiqs.com/results/black_lives_matter?uncertainty=true&annotations=true&zoomIn=true
256. civiqs.com/results/gun_control?uncertainty=true&annotations=true&zoomIn=true
257. civiqs.com/results/favorable_democrats?uncertainty=true&annotations=true&zoomIn=true
258. civiqs.com/results/cannabis_legal?uncertainty=true&annotations=true&zoomIn=true
259. civiqs.com/results/immigrants_citizenship?uncertainty=true&annotations=true&zoomIn=true
260. civiqs.com/results/raise_taxes_wealthy?uncertainty=true&annotations=true&zoomIn=true

261. civiqs.com/results/environment_protect?uncertainty=true&annotations=true&zoomIn=true
262. civiqs.com/results/medicare_for_all?uncertainty=true&annotations=true&zoomIn=true
263. civiqs.com/results/universal_basic_income?uncertainty=true&annotations=true&zoomIn=true
264. civiqs.com/results/job_guarantee?uncertainty=true&annotations=true&zoomIn=true
265. amzn.to/3Mq3x7t
266. libertyblock.com/which-state-has-the-most-freedom
267. amzn.to/3aV9cnN
268. amzn.to/3K2452d
269. libertyblock.com/divorce-dc

Made in the USA
Middletown, DE
23 June 2023